INTRODUCTION

LANGUAGE AND GRAMMAR

I. The Nature of Language

Language is the expression of thought by means of spoken or written words.

The English word *language* comes (through the French *langue*) from the Latin *lingua*, "the tongue." But the tongue is not the only organ used in speaking. The lips, the teeth, the roof of the mouth, the soft palate (or uvula), the nose, and the vocal chords all help to produce the sounds of which language consists. These various organs make up one delicate and complicated piece of mechanism upon which the breath of the speaker acts like that of a musician upon a clarinet or other wind instrument.

Spoken language, then, is composed of a great variety of sounds made with the vocal organs. A word may consist of one sound (as *Ah!* or *O* or *I*), but most words consist of two or more different sounds (as *go, see, try, finish*). Long or short, however, a word is merely a sign made to express thought.

Thought may be imperfectly expressed by signs made with the head, the hands, etc. Thus, if I grasp a person's arm and point to a dog, he may understand me to ask, "Do you see that dog?" And his nod in reply may stand for "Yes, I see him." But any dialogue carried on in this way must be both fragmentary and uncertain. To express our thoughts fully, freely, and accurately, we must use words,—that is, signs made with the voice. Such voice-signs have had meanings associated with them by custom or tradition,

so that their sense is at once understood by all. Their advantage is twofold: they are far more numerous and varied than other signs; and the meanings attached to them are much more definite than those of nods and gestures.

Written words are signs made with the pen to represent and recall to the mind the spoken words (or voice-signs). Written language (that is, composition) must, of necessity, be somewhat fuller than spoken language, as well as more formal and exact. For the reader's understanding is not assisted by the tones of the voice, the changing expressions of the face, and the lively gestures, which help to make spoken language intelligible.

Most words are the signs of definite ideas. Thus, *Charles, captain, cat, mouse, bread, stone, cup, ink,* call up images or pictures of persons or things; *strike, dive, climb, dismount,* express particular kinds of action; *green, blue, careless, rocky, triangular, muscular,* enable us to describe objects with accuracy. Even general terms like *goodness, truth, courage, cowardice, generosity,* have sufficiently precise meanings, for they name qualities, or traits of character, with which everybody is familiar.

By the use of such words, even when not combined in groups, we can express our thoughts much more satisfactorily than by mere gestures. The utterance of the single word "Charles!" may signify: "Hullo, Charles! are you here? I am surprised to see you." "Bread!" may suggest to the hearer: "Give me bread! I am very hungry." "Courage!" may be almost equivalent to, "Don't be down-hearted! Your troubles will soon be over."

Language, however, is not confined to the utterance of single words. To express our thoughts we must put words together,—we must combine them into groups; and such groups have settled meanings (just as words have), established (like the meanings of single words) by the customs or habits of the particular language that we are speaking or writing. Further, these groups are not thrown together haphazard. We must construct them in accordance with certain fixed rules. Otherwise we shall fail to express ourselves clearly and acceptably, and we may even succeed in saying the opposite of what we mean.

In constructing these groups (which we call **phrases**, **clauses**, and **sentences**) we have the aid of a large number of short words like *and, if, by, to, in, is, was*, which are very different from the definite and picturesque words that we have just examined. They do not call up distinct images in the mind, and we should find it hard to define any of them. Yet their importance in the expression of thought is clear; for they serve to join other words together, and to show their relation to each other in those groups which make up connected speech.

Thus, "box heavy" conveys some meaning; but "*The* box *is* heavy" is a clear and definite statement. *The* shows that some particular box is meant, and *is* enables us to make an assertion about it. *And*, in "Charles and John are my brothers," indicates that Charles and John are closely connected in my thought, and that what I say of one applies also to the other. *If*, in "If Charles comes, I shall be glad to see him," connects two statements, and shows that one of them is a mere supposition (for Charles may or may not come).

In grouping words, our language has three different ways of indicating their relations: (1) the forms of the words themselves; (2) their order; (3) the use of little words like *and, if, is*, etc.

I. **Change of form.** Words may change their form. Thus the word *boy* becomes *boys* when more than one is meant; *kill* becomes *killed* when past time is referred to; *was* becomes *were* when we are speaking of two or more persons or things; *fast* becomes *faster* when a higher degree of speed is indicated. Such change of form is called **inflection**, and the word is said to be **inflected**.

Inflection is an important means of showing the relations of words in connected speech. In "Henry's racket weighs fourteen ounces," the form *Henry's* shows at once the relation between Henry and the racket,—namely, that Henry owns or possesses it. The word *Henry*, then, may change its form to *Henry's* to indicate ownership or possession.

II. **Order of words.** In "John struck Charles," the way in which the words are arranged shows who it was that struck, and who received the blow. Change the order of words to "Charles struck John," and the meaning is reversed. It is, then, the **order** that shows the relation of *John* to *struck*, and of *struck* to *Charles*.

III. **Use of other words.** Compare the two sentences:

> The train *from* Boston has just arrived.
> The train *for* Boston has just arrived.

Here *from* and *for* show the relation between the *train* and *Boston*. "The Boston train" might mean either the train *from* Boston or the train *for* Boston. By using *from* or *for* we make the sense unmistakable.

Two matters, then, are of vital importance in language,—the forms of words, and the relations of words. The science which treats of these two matters is called **grammar**.

Inflection is a change in the form of a word indicating some change in its meaning.

The relation in which a word stands to other words in the sentence is called its construction.

Grammar is the science which treats of the forms and the constructions of words.

Syntax is that department of grammar which treats of the constructions of words.

Grammar, then, may be said to concern itself with two main subjects,—inflection and syntax.

English belongs to a family of languages—the Indo-European Family[1]—which is rich in forms of inflection. This richness may be seen in other members of the family,—such as Greek or Latin. The Latin word *homo*, "man," for example, has eight different inflectional forms,—*homo*, "a man"; *hominis*, "of a man"; *homini*, "to a man," and so on. Thus, in Latin, the grammatical construction of a word is, in general, shown by that particular inflectional ending (or termination) which it has in any particular sentence. In the Anglo-Saxon period,[2] English was likewise well furnished with such inflectional endings, though not so abundantly as Latin. Many of these, however, had disappeared by Chaucer's time (1340–1400), and still others have since been lost, so that modern English is one of the least inflected of languages. Such losses are not to be lamented. By due attention to the order of words, and by using *of, to, for, from, in*, and the like, we can express all the relations denoted by the ancient inflections. The gain in simplicity is enormous.

II. GRAMMAR AND USAGE

Since language is the expression of thought, the rules of grammar agree, in the main, with the laws of thought. In other words, grammar is usually logical,—that is, its rules accord, in general, with the principles of logic, which is the science of exact reasoning.

The rules of grammar, however, do not derive their authority from logic, but from good usage,—that is, from the customs or habits followed by educated speakers and writers. These customs, of course, differ among different nations, and every language has therefore its own stock of peculiar constructions or turns of expression. Such peculiarities are called **idioms**.

Thus, in English we say, "It is I"; but in French the idiom is "C'est moi," which corresponds to "It is me." Many careless speakers of English follow the French idiom in this particular, but their practice has not yet come to be the accepted usage. Hence, though "C'est moi" is correct in French, we must still regard "It is me" as ungrammatical in English. It would, however, become correct if it should ever be adopted by the great majority of educated persons.

Grammar does not enact laws for the conduct of speech. Its business is to ascertain and set forth those customs of language which have the sanction of good usage. If good usage changes, the rules of grammar must change. If two forms or constructions are in good use, the grammarian must admit them both. Occasionally, also, there is room for difference of opinion. These facts, however, do not lessen the authority of grammar in the case of any cultivated language. For in such a language usage is so well settled in almost every particular as to enable the grammarian to say positively what is right and what is wrong. Even in matters of divided usage, it is seldom difficult to determine which of two forms or constructions is preferred by careful writers.

Every language has two standards of usage,—the colloquial and the literary. By "colloquial language," we mean the language of conversation; by "literary language," that employed in literary composition. Everyday colloquial English admits many words, forms, phrases, and constructions that would be out of place in a dignified essay. On the other hand, it is an error in taste to be always "talking like a book." Unpractised speakers and writers should, however, be conservative. They should avoid, even in informal talk, any word or expression that is of doubtful propriety. Only those who know what they are about, can venture to take liberties. It is quite possible to be correct without being stilted or affected.[3]

Every living language is constantly changing. Words, forms, and constructions become **obsolete** (that is, go out of use) and others take their places. Consequently, one often notes in the older English classics, methods of expression which, though formerly correct, are ungrammatical now. Here a twofold caution is necessary. On the one hand, we must not criticise Shakspere or Chaucer for using the English of his own time; but, on the other hand, we must not try to defend our own errors by appealing to ancient usage.

Examples of constructions once in good use, but no longer admissible, are: "the best of the two" (for "the better of the two"); "the most unkindest cut of all"; "There's two or three of us" (for *there are*); "I have forgot the map" (for *forgotten*); "Every one of these letters are in my name" (for *is*); "I think it be" (for *is*).

The language of poetry admits many old words, forms, and constructions that are no longer used in ordinary prose. These are called **archaisms** (that is, ancient expressions). Among the commonest archaisms are *thou, ye, hath, thinkest, doth*. Such forms are also common in prose, in what is known as the **solemn style**, which is modelled, in great part, on the language of the Bible.[4]

In general, it should be remembered that the style which one uses should be appropriate,—that is, it should fit the occasion. A short story and a scientific exposition will differ in style; a familiar letter will naturally shun the formalities of business or legal correspondence. Good style is not a necessary result of grammatical correctness, but without such correctness it is, of course, impossible.

SUMMARY OF GENERAL PRINCIPLES

1. Language is the expression of thought by means of spoken or written words.

2. Words are the signs of ideas.

Spoken words are signs made with the vocal organs; written words are signs made with the pen to represent the spoken words.

The meanings of these signs are settled by custom or tradition in each language.

3. Most words are the signs of definite ideas: as,—*Charles, captain, cat, strike, dive, climb, triangular, careless.*

Other words, of less definite meaning, serve to connect the more definite words and to show their relations to each other in connected speech.

4. In the expression of thought, words are combined into groups called phrases, clauses, and sentences.

5. The relation in which a word stands to other words in the sentence is called its construction.

The construction of English words is shown in three ways: (1) by their form; (2) by their order; (3) by the use of other words like *to, from, is,* etc.

6. Inflection is a change in the form of a word indicating some change in its meaning: as,—*boy, boy's*; *man, men*; *drink, drank.*

7. Grammar is the science which treats of the forms and the constructions of words.

Syntax is that department of grammar which treats of the constructions of words.

8. The rules of grammar derive their authority from good usage,—that is, from the customs or habits followed by educated speakers and writers.

PART ONE
THE PARTS OF SPEECH IN THE SENTENCE

Summary. The Sentence: Subject and Predicate; Kinds of Sentences.—Use of words in the Sentence: the Eight Parts of Speech; Infinitives and Participles.—Comparative Importance of the Parts of Speech in the Sentence: the Subject Noun (or Simple Subject); the Predicate Verb (or Simple Predicate); Compound Subject and Predicate.—Substitutes for the Parts of Speech: Phrases; Clauses; Compound and Complex Sentences.

THE SENTENCE

1. A sentence is a group of words which expresses a complete thought.

Fire burns.

Wolves howl.

Rain is falling.

Charles is courageous.

Patient effort removes mountains.

London is the largest city in the world.

A man who respects himself should never condescend to use slovenly language.

Some of these sentences are short, expressing a very simple thought; others are comparatively long, because the thought is more complicated and therefore requires more words for its expression. But every one of them, whether short or long, is complete in itself. It comes to a definite end, and is followed by a full pause.

2. Every sentence, whether short or long, consists of two parts,—a **subject** and a **predicate**.

The subject of a sentence designates the person, place, or thing that is spoken of; the predicate is that which is said of the subject.

> Thus, in the first example in §_1, the subject is *fire* and the predicate is *burns*. In the third, the subject is *rain*; the predicate, *is falling*. In the last, the subject is *a man who respects himself*; the predicate, *should never condescend to use slovenly language*.

Either the subject or the predicate may consist of a single word or of a number of words. But neither the subject by itself nor the predicate by itself, however extended, is a sentence. The mere mention of a thing (*fire*) does not express a complete thought. Neither does a mere assertion (*burns*), if we neglect to mention the person or thing about which the assertion is made. Thus it appears that both a subject and a predicate are necessary to make a sentence.

3. Sentences may be declarative, interrogative, imperative, or exclamatory.

1. **A declarative sentence declares or asserts something as a fact.**

   Dickens wrote "David Copperfield."
   The army approached the city.

2. **An interrogative sentence asks a question.**

   Who is that officer?
   Does Arthur Moore live here?

3. **An imperative sentence expresses a command or a request.**

   Open the window.
   Pronounce the vowels more distinctly.

4. **An exclamatory sentence expresses surprise, grief, or some other emotion in the form of an exclamation or cry.**

> How calm the sea is!
> What a noise the engine makes!

A declarative, an interrogative, or an imperative sentence is also **exclamatory**, if it is uttered in an intense or excited tone of voice.

4. In imperative sentences, the subject (*thou* or *you*) is almost always omitted, because it is **understood** by both speaker and hearer without being expressed.

> Such omitted words, which are present (*in idea*) to the minds of both speaker and hearer, are said to be "understood." Thus, in "Open the window," the subject is "*you* (understood)." If expressed, the subject would be emphatic: as,—"*You* open the window."

5. The subject of a sentence commonly precedes the predicate, but sometimes the predicate precedes.

> Here comes Tom.
> Next came Edward.
> Over went the carriage.

A sentence in which the predicate precedes the subject is said to be in the **inverted order**. This order is especially common in interrogative sentences.

> Where is your boat?
> When was your last birthday?
> Whither wander you?—SHAKSPERE.

THE PARTS OF SPEECH

6. If we examine the words in any sentence, we observe that they have different tasks or duties to perform in the expression of thought.

Savage beasts roamed through the forest.

In this sentence, *beasts* and *forest* are the **names** of objects; *roamed* **asserts action**, telling us what the beasts *did*; *savage* **describes** the beasts; *through* shows the **relation** in thought between *forest* and *roamed*; *the* **limits** the meaning of *forest*, showing that one particular forest is meant. Thus each of these words has its **special office** (or **function**) **in the sentence**.

7. In accordance with their use in the sentence, words are divided into eight classes called parts of speech,—namely, nouns, pronouns, adjectives, verbs, adverbs, prepositions, conjunctions, and interjections.

I. NOUNS

8. A noun is the name of a person, place, or thing.

EXAMPLES: Lincoln, William, Elizabeth, sister, engineer, Chicago, island, shelf, star, window, happiness, anger, sidewalk, courage, loss, song.

II. PRONOUNS

9. A pronoun is a word used instead of a noun. It designates a person, place, or thing without naming it.

In "*I* am ready," the pronoun *I* is a convenient substitute for the speaker's name. In "*You* have forgotten *your* umbrella," the pronouns *you* and *your* designate the person to whom one is speaking.

Other pronouns are: *he, his, him; she, hers, her; it, its; this, that; who, whose, whom, which; myself, yourself, himself, themselves.*

Since pronouns stand for nouns, they enable us to talk about a person, place, or thing without constantly repeating the name.

10. Nouns and pronouns are called substantives.

Nouns and pronouns are very similar in their use. The difference between them is merely that the noun designates a person, place, or thing by **naming** it, and that the pronoun **designates**, but does not **name**. Hence it is convenient to have a general term (**substantive**) to include both these parts of speech.

11. The substantive to which a pronoun refers is called its antecedent.

Frank introduced the boys to *his* father. [*Frank* is the antecedent of the pronoun *his*.]

Eleanor is visiting *her* aunt.

The *book* has lost *its* cover.

The *trappers* sat round *their* camp fire.

Washington and *Franklin* served *their* country in different ways. [*Their* has two antecedents, connected by *and*.]

III. ADJECTIVES

12. An adjective is a word which describes or limits a substantive.[5]

This it usually does by indicating some quality.

An adjective is said to belong to the substantive which it describes or limits.

13. An adjective limits a substantive by restricting the range of its meaning.

The noun *box*, for example, includes a great variety of objects. If we say *wooden* box, we exclude boxes of metal, of paper, etc. If we use a second adjective (*small*) and a third (*square*), we limit the size and the shape of the box.

Most adjectives (like *wooden, square,* and *small*) **describe** as well as limit. Such words are called **descriptive adjectives**.

We may, however, limit the noun *box* to a single specimen by means of the adjective *this* or *that* or *the,* which does not **describe**, but simply points out, or **designates**. Such words are called **definitive adjectives**.[6]

IV. VERBS

14. A verb is a word which can assert something (usually an action) concerning a person, place, or thing.[7]

> The wind *blows.*
> The horses *ran.*
> The fire *blazed.*
> Her jewels *sparkled.*
> Tom *climbed* a tree.
> The dynamite *exploded.*

Some verbs express state or condition rather than action.

> The treaty still *exists.*
> The book *lies* on the table.
> Near the church *stood* an elm.
> My aunt *suffers* much from headache.

15. A group of words may be needed, instead of a single verb, to make an assertion.

A group of words that is used as a verb is called a verb-phrase.

You *will see.*

The tree *has fallen.*

We *might have invited* her.

Our driver *has been discharged.*

16. Certain verbs, when used to make verb-phrases, are called **auxiliary** (that is, "aiding") **verbs**, because they help other verbs to express action or state of some particular kind.

> Thus, in "You *will see,*" the auxiliary verb *will* helps *see* to express **future** action; in "We *might have invited* her," the auxiliaries *might* and *have* help *invited* to express action that was **possible** in past time.

The auxiliary verbs are *is* (*are, was, were,* etc.), *may, can, must, might, shall, will, could, would, should, have, had, do, did.* Their forms and uses will be studied in connection with the inflection of verbs.

The auxiliary verb regularly comes first in a verb-phrase, and may be separated from the rest of it by some other word or words.

> Where *was* Washington *born*?
>
> The boat *was* slowly but steadily *approaching.*

17. *Is* (in its various forms) and several other verbs may be used to frame sentences in which some word or words in the predicate describe or define the subject.

1. Gold *is* a metal.
2. Charles *is* my friend's name.
3. The colors of this butterfly *are* brilliant.
4. Iron *becomes* red in the fire.
5. Our condition *seemed* desperate.
6. Bertram *proved* a good friend in this emergency.

7. My soul *grows* sad with troubles.—SHAKSPERE.

In the first sentence, the verb *is* not only **makes an assertion**, but it also **connects** the rest of the predicate (*a metal*) with the subject (*gold*) in such a way that *a metal* serves as a description or definition of *gold*.

In sentences 4–7, *becomes, seemed, proved,* and *grows* are similarly used.

In such sentences *is* and other verbs that are used for the same purpose are called **copulative** (that is, "joining") **verbs**.

> *Is* in this use is often called the **copula**, that is, the "joiner" or "link."

The forms of the verb *is* are very irregular. Among the commonest are: *am, is, are, was, were,* and the verb-phrases *has been, have been, had been, shall be, will be.*[8]

V. ADVERBS

18. An adverb is a word which modifies a verb, an adjective, or another adverb.

> To **modify** a word is to change or affect its meaning in some way. Thus in "The river fell *rapidly,*" the adverb *rapidly* modifies the verb *fell* by showing *how* the falling took place. In "I am *never* late," "This is *absolutely* true," "That is *too* bad," the italicized words are adverbs modifying adjectives; in "He came *very* often," "He spoke *almost* hopefully," "The river fell *too* rapidly," they are adverbs modifying other adverbs.

Most adverbs answer the question "How?" "When?" "Where?" or "To what degree or extent?"

19. Observe that adverbs modify verbs in much the same way in which adjectives modify nouns.

ADJECTIVES	ADVERBS

A *bright* fire burned.	The fire burned *brightly*.
A *fierce* wind blew.	The wind blew *fiercely*.

A word or group of words that changes or modifies the meaning of another word is called a modifier.

Adjectives and adverbs, then, are both **modifiers**. Adjectives modify substantives; adverbs modify verbs, adjectives, or other adverbs.

VI. PREPOSITIONS

20. A preposition is a word placed before a substantive to show its relation to some other word in the sentence.

The substantive which follows a preposition is called its object.

A preposition is said to **govern** its object.

> In "The surface *of* the water glistened," *of* makes it clear that *surface* belongs with *water*. In "Philip is *on* the river," *on* shows Philip's position with respect to the river. *In*, or *near*, or *beyond* would have indicated a different relation. *Water* is the object of the preposition *of*, and *river* is the object of the preposition *on*.

21. A preposition often has more than one object.

> Over *hill* and *dale* he ran.
> He was filled with *shame* and *despair*.

VII. CONJUNCTIONS

22. A conjunction connects words or groups of words.

A conjunction differs from a preposition in having no object, and in indicating a less definite relation between the words which it connects.

> In "Time *and* tide wait for no man," "The parcel was small *but* heavy," "He wore a kind of doublet *or* jacket," the conjunctions *and, but, or*, connect single words,—*time* with *tide*, *small* with *heavy*, *doublet* with *jacket*. In "Do not go *if* you are afraid," "I came

because you sent for me," "Take my key, *but* do not lose it," "Sweep the floor *and* dust the furniture," each conjunction connects the entire group of words preceding it with the entire group following it.

VIII. INTERJECTIONS

23. An interjection is a cry or other exclamatory sound expressing surprise, anger, pleasure, or some other emotion or feeling.

Interjections usually have no grammatical connection with the groups of words in which they stand; hence their name, which means "thrown in."

EXAMPLES: *Oh!* I forgot. *Ah*, how I miss you! *Bravo! Alas!*

THE SAME WORD AS DIFFERENT PARTS OF SPEECH

24. The meaning of a word in the sentence determines to what part of speech it belongs.

The same word may be sometimes one part of speech, sometimes another.

Words of entirely separate origin, meaning, and use sometimes look and sound alike: as in "The minstrel sang a plaintive *lay*," and "He *lay* on the ground." But the following examples (§ 25) show that the same word may have more than one kind of grammatical office (or function). It is the **meaning** which we give to a word **in the sentence** that determines its classification as a part of speech.

25. The chief classes of words thus variously used are (1) nouns and adjectives, (2) nouns and verbs, (3) adjectives and adverbs, (4) adjectives and pronouns, (5) adverbs and prepositions.

I. NOUNS AND ADJECTIVES

NOUNS	ADJECTIVES

Rubber comes from South America.	This wheel has a *rubber* tire.
That *brick* is yellow.	Here is a *brick* house.
The *rich* have a grave responsibility.	A *rich* merchant lives here.

The first two examples show how words that are commonly nouns may be used as adjectives; the third shows how words that are commonly adjectives may be used as nouns.

II. Nouns and Verbs

Nouns	Verbs
Hear the *wash* of the tide.	*Wash* those windows.
Give me a *stamp*.	*Stamp* this envelope.
It is the *call* of the sea.	Ye *call* me chief.

Other examples are: act, address, ally, answer, boast, care, cause, close, defeat, doubt, drop, heap, hope, mark, offer, pile, place, rest, rule, sail, shape, sleep, spur, test, watch, wound.

III. Adjectives and Adverbs

Adjectives	Adverbs
That is a *fast* boat.	The snow is melting *fast*.
Draw a *straight* line.	The arrow flew *straight*.
Early comers get good seats.	Tom awoke *early*.

For an explanation of the form of these adverbs, see § 191.

IV. Adjectives and Pronouns

Adjectives	Pronouns

This man looks unhappy.	*This* is the sergeant.
That book is a dictionary.	*That* is a kangaroo.
Each day brings its opportunity.	I received a dollar from *each*.

For further study of this class of words, see pp. 62–65.

V. ADVERBS AND PREPOSITIONS

ADVERBS	PREPOSITIONS
Jill came tumbling *after*.	He returned *after* the accident.
We went *below*.	*Below* us lay the valley.
The weeds sprang *up*.	We walked *up* the hill.

Other examples are: aboard, before, beyond, down, inside, underneath.

Miscellaneous examples of variation are the following:—

NOUN.	The *calm* lasted for three days.
ADJECTIVE.	*Calm* words show quiet minds.
VERB.	*Calm* your angry friend.

Other examples are: iron, stone, paper, sugar, salt, bark, quiet, black, light, head, wet, round, square, winter, spring.

NOUN.	*Wrong* seldom prospers.
ADJECTIVE.	You have taken the *wrong* road.
ADVERB.	Edward often spells words *wrong*.
VERB.	You *wrong* me by your suspicions.
NOUN.	The *outside* of the castle is gloomy.

ADJECTIVE.	We have an *outside* stateroom.
ADVERB.	The messenger is waiting *outside*.
PREPOSITION.	I shall ride *outside* the coach.
ADJECTIVE.	*That* boat is a sloop.
PRONOUN.	*That* is my uncle.
CONJUNCTION.	You said *that* you would help me.
ADJECTIVE.	*Neither* road leads to Utica.
PRONOUN.	*Neither* of us arrived in time.
CONJUNCTION.	*Neither* Tom nor I was late.
PREPOSITION.	I am waiting *for* the train.
CONJUNCTION.	You have plenty of time, *for* the train is late.
INTERJECTION.	*Hurrah!* the battle is won.
NOUN.	I heard a loud *hurrah*.
VERB.	The enemy flees. Our men *hurrah*.

INFINITIVES AND PARTICIPLES

26. Two classes of verb-forms illustrate in a striking way the fact that the same word may belong to different parts of speech; for they really belong to two different parts of speech at one and the same time. These are the **infinitive** (which is both **verb** and **noun**) and the **participle** (which is both **verb** and **adjective**).

27. Examples of the **infinitive** may be seen in the following sentences:

To struggle was useless.

To escape is impossible.

To exercise regularly preserves the health.

To struggle is clearly a **noun**, for (1) it is the subject of the sentence, and (2) the noun *effort* or *exertion* might be put in the place of *to struggle*.

Similarly, the noun *escape* might be substituted for *to escape*; and, in the third sentence, *regular exercise* (a noun modified by an adjective) might be substituted for *to exercise regularly*.

But these three forms (*to struggle, to escape,* and *to exercise*) are also **verbs**, for they express action, and one of them (*to exercise*) is modified by an adverb (*regularly*). Such forms, therefore, are noun-forms of the verb. They are classed with verbs, and are called **infinitives**.

28. The infinitive is a verb-form which partakes of the nature of a noun. It is commonly preceded by the preposition *to*, which is called the sign of the infinitive.

29. The infinitive without *to* is used in a great variety of verb-phrases.

> I *shall go.*
> John *will win.*
> Mary *may recite.*
> Jack *can swim.*

Such phrases will be studied in connection with the inflection of verbs.

NOTE. That *go, win, recite,* and *swim* are infinitives may be seen by comparing the following sentences:—"I intend *to go*," "John is sure *to win*," "Mary is permitted *to recite*," "Jack is able *to swim*."

30. The following sentence contains two **participles**:—

> *Shattered* and slowly *sinking*, the frigate drifted out to sea.

In this sentence, we recognize *shattered* as a form of the **verb** *shatter*, and *sinking* as a form of the **verb** *sink*. They both express action, and *sinking* is modified by the adverb *slowly*. But *shattered* and *sinking* have also the nature of **adjectives**, for they are used to describe the noun *frigate*. Such words, then, are adjective forms of the verb. They are classed as verbs, and are called **participles**, because they share (or participate in) the nature of adjectives.

31. The participle is a verb-form which has no subject, but which partakes of the nature of an adjective and expresses action or state in such a way as to describe or limit a substantive.

A participle is said to **belong to** the substantive which it describes or limits.

32. The chief classes of participles are **present participles** and **past participles**, so called from the time which they denote.

All present participles end in *ing*. Past participles have several different endings, which will be studied in connection with the inflection of verbs (§ 334).

33. Participles are used in a variety of verb-phrases.

> Tom *is coming*.
> Our boat *was wrecked*.
> I *have sent* the money.
> He *has brought* me a letter.
> Your book *is found*.
> They *have sold* their horses.
> You *have broken* your watch.
> The ship *had struck* on the reef.

Such phrases will be studied in connection with the inflection of verbs.

NOTE. The double nature of the infinitive (as both verb and noun) and the participle (as both verb and adjective) almost justifies one in classifying each as a distinct part of speech (so as to make ten parts of speech instead of eight). But it is more convenient to include them under the head of verbs, in accordance with the usual practice.

SIMPLE AND COMPLETE SUBJECT AND PREDICATE

34. Our survey of the eight parts of speech has shown, (1) that these have very different offices or functions in the sentence, and (2) that their functions are not of equal importance.

Clearly, the most important parts of speech are **substantives** (nouns and pronouns) and **verbs**.

Substantives enable us to **name or designate** persons, places, or things, and verbs enable us to **make statements** about them. Both substantives and verbs, then, are absolutely necessary in framing sentences. Without a substantive, there can be no **subject**; without a verb, there can be no **predicate**: and both a subject and a predicate, as we have seen, are needed to make a sentence.

Adjectives and **adverbs** are less important than substantives and verbs. Their function is to **modify** other parts of speech, that is, to change their meaning in some way. Thus adjectives modify substantives (by describing or limiting), and adverbs usually modify verbs (by indicating *how, when*, or *where* the action took place). Without substantives, there would be no use for adjectives; without verbs, there would be little use for adverbs.

Prepositions and **conjunctions** are also less important than substantives and verbs. Their office is to connect and to show relation. Of course, there would be no place for connectives if there were nothing to connect.

Interjections are the least important of all. They add liveliness to language, but they are not actual necessities. We could express all the thoughts that enter our minds without ever using an interjection.

35. A sentence may consist of but two words,—a noun or pronoun (the subject) and a verb (the predicate). Thus,—

Charles | swims.

Commonly, however, either the subject or the predicate, or both, will contain more than one word. Thus,—

Young Charles | swims slowly.

Here the **complete subject** (*young Charles*) consists of a noun (*Charles*) and an adjective (*young*), which describes *Charles*. The **complete predicate** consists of a verb (*swims*) and an adverb (*slowly*), which modifies *swim* by indicating *how* the action is performed. The subject noun (*Charles*) and the predicate verb (*swims*) are the chief words in the sentence, for neither could be omitted without destroying it. They form, so to speak, the frame or skeleton of the whole. Either of the two modifiers, the adjective or the adverb, or both, might be omitted, without destroying the sentence; for this would still exist as the expression of a thought (*Charles swims*), though the thought would be less definite and exact than it is when the modifiers are included.

36. The simple subject of a sentence is a noun or pronoun.

The simple predicate of a sentence is a verb or verb-phrase.

The simple subject, with such words as explain or complete its meaning, forms the complete subject.

The simple predicate, with such words as explain or complete its meaning, forms the complete predicate.

In each of the following sentences the **complete subject** and the **complete predicate** are separated by a vertical line, and the **simple subject** and the **simple predicate** are printed in italics:—

The *spider* | *spreads* her web.
The fiery *smoke* | *rose* upward in billowing volumes.

A nameless *unrest* | *urged* me forward.

Our frantic *horses* | *swept* round an angle of the road.

The *infirmities* of age | *came* early upon him.

The general *feeling* among the English in Bengal | *was* strongly in favor of the Governor General.

Salutes | *were fired* from the batteries.

The *Clives* | *had been settled* ever since the twelfth century on an estate of no great value near Market Drayton in Shropshire.

I | *have written* repeatedly to Mr. Hobhouse.

37. Two or more simple subjects may be joined to make one **compound subject**, and two or more simple predicates to make one **compound predicate**.

1. *Charles* and *Henry* | play tennis well.
2. *Moore* and *I* | passed some merry days together.
3. *Frances* and *she* | are friends.
4. *Hats, caps, boots,* and *gloves* | were piled together in confusion.
5. The watch | *sank* and *was lost.*
6. The balloon | *rose* higher and higher and finally *disappeared.*
7. He | neither *smiled* nor *frowned.*
8. *Snow* and *ice* | *covered* the ground and *made* our progress difficult.

38. A compound subject or predicate consists of two or more simple subjects or predicates, joined, when necessary, by conjunctions.

Either the subject or the predicate, or both, may be compound.

In the first example in § 37, two simple subjects (*Charles* and *Henry*) are joined by the conjunction *and* to make a compound subject. In the fourth, four substantives (*hats*, *caps*, *boots*, *gloves*) form a series in which the last two are joined by *and*. In the fifth, sixth, and seventh, the predicates are compound; in the eighth, both the subject and the predicate.

39. The following conjunctions may be used to join the members of a compound subject or predicate: *and* (*both ... and*), *or* (*either ... or*; *whether ... or*), *nor* (*neither ... nor*).

SUBSTITUTES FOR PARTS OF SPEECH

PHRASES

40. A group of words may take the place of a part of speech

> *The Father of Waters* is the Mississippi.
> A girl *with blue eyes* stood *at the window*.
> You *are looking* well.

The Father of Waters is used as a noun, since it names something.
With blue eyes takes the place of an adjective (*blue-eyed*), and modifies *girl*.
At the window indicates, as an adverb might, where the girl stood, and modifies *stood*.
Are looking could be replaced by the verb *look*.

41. A group of connected words, not containing a subject and a predicate, is called a phrase.

A phrase is often equivalent to a part of speech.

1. A phrase used as a noun is called a **noun-phrase**.
2. A phrase used as a verb is called a **verb-phrase**.
3. A phrase used as an adjective is called an **adjective phrase**.
4. A phrase used as an adverb is called an **adverbial phrase**.

In the examples in § 40, *The Father of Waters* is a noun-phrase; *with blue eyes*, an adjective phrase; *at the window*, an adverbial phrase; *are looking*, a verb-phrase.

42. Many adjective and adverbial phrases consist of a **preposition and its object**, with or without other words.

> Your umbrella is *in the corner.*
> He has a heart *of oak.*
> A cup *with a broken handle* stood *on the shelf.*
> My house *of cards* fell *to the floor in a heap.*

Adjective or adverbial phrases consisting of a preposition and its object, with or without other words, may be called prepositional phrases.

CLAUSES—COMPOUND AND COMPLEX SENTENCES

43. Phrases must be carefully distinguished from **clauses**. The difference is that a clause contains a subject and a predicate and a phrase does not.

44. A clause is a group of words that forms part of a sentence and that contains a subject and a predicate.

> The lightning flashed | and | the thunder roared.
> The train started | when the bell rang.

Each of these sentences contains two clauses; but the relation between the clauses in the first sentence is very different from that between the clauses in the second.

In the first example, each of the two clauses makes a separate and distinct statement, and might stand by itself as a simple sentence,—that is, as a sentence having but one subject and one predicate. These clauses are joined by the conjunction *and,* which is not a part of either. No doubt the speaker feels that there is some relation in thought between the two statements, or he would not have put them together as clauses in the same sentence. But there is nothing in the form of expression to show what that relation is. In other words, the two clauses are grammatically **independent**, for neither of them modifies (or affects the meaning of) the other. The clauses are therefore said to be **coördinate**,—that is, of the same "order" or rank, and the sentence is called **compound**.

In the second example, on the contrary, the relation between the two clauses is indicated with precision. One clause (*the train started*) makes the main statement,—it expresses the chief fact. Hence it is called the **main** (or **principal**) **clause**. The other clause (*when the bell rang*) is added because the speaker wishes to **modify** the main verb (*started*) by defining the time of the action. This clause, then, is used as a **part of speech**. Its function is the same as that of an adverb (*promptly*) or an adverbial phrase (*on the stroke of the bell*). For this purpose alone it exists, and not as an independent statement. Hence it is called a **dependent** (or **subordinate**) **clause**, because it **depends** (that is, "hangs") upon the main clause, and so occupies a lower or "subordinate" rank in the sentence. When thus constructed, a sentence is said to be **complex**.

45. An ordinary **compound sentence** (as we have seen in § 44) is made by joining two or more simple sentences, each of which thus becomes an **independent coördinate clause**.

In the same way we may join two or more **complex sentences**, using them as clauses to make one compound sentence:—

> The train started when the bell rang, | and | Tom watched until the last car disappeared.

This sentence is manifestly **compound**, for it consists of two **coördinate clauses** (*the train started when the bell rang*; *Tom watched until the last car* *disappeared*) joined by *and*. Each of these two clauses is itself **complex**, for each could stand by itself as a complex sentence.

Similarly, a **complex** and a **simple** sentence may be joined as coördinate clauses to make a compound sentence.

> The train started when the bell rang, | and | Tom gazed after it in despair.

Such a sentence, which is **compound in its structure**, but in which one or more of the coördinate clauses are **complex**, is called a **compound complex sentence**.[9]

46. A clause is a group of words that forms part of a sentence and that contains a subject and a predicate.

A clause used as a part of speech is called a subordinate clause. All other clauses are said to be independent.

Clauses of the same order or rank are said to be coördinate.

Sentences may be simple, compound, or complex.

1. A simple sentence has but one subject and one predicate, either or both of which may be compound.

2. A compound sentence consists of two or more independent coördinate clauses, which may or may not be joined by conjunctions.

3. A complex sentence consists of two or more clauses, one of which is independent and the rest subordinate.

A compound sentence in which one or more of the coördinate clauses are complex is called a compound complex sentence.

I. Simple Sentences

Iron rusts.

George V is king.

Dogs, foxes, and hares are quadrupeds. [Compound subject.]

The defendant rose and addressed the court. [Compound predicate.]

Merton and his men crossed the bridge and scaled the wall. [Both subject and predicate are compound.]

II. Compound Sentences

Shakspere was born in 1564; he died in 1616. [Two coördinate clauses; no conjunction.]

A rifle cracked, and the wolf fell dead. [Two clauses joined by the conjunction *and*.]

You must hurry, or we shall lose the train. [Two clauses joined by *or*.]

James Watt did not invent the steam engine, but he greatly improved it. [Two clauses joined by *but*.]

Either you have neglected to write or your letter has failed to reach me. [Two clauses joined by *either ... or*.]

The following conjunctions may be used to join coördinate clauses: *and* (*both ... and*), *or* (*either ... or*), *nor* (*neither ... nor*), *but, for.*

III. Complex Sentences

Examples will be found in §§ 48–50.

Clauses as Parts of Speech

47. Subordinate clauses, like phrases, are used as **parts of speech**. They serve as substitutes for **nouns**, for **adjectives**, or for **adverbs**.

1. A subordinate clause that is used as a noun is called a noun (or substantive) clause.

2. A subordinate clause that modifies a substantive is called an adjective clause.

3. A subordinate clause that serves as an adverbial modifier is called an adverbial clause.

48. I. Noun (or Substantive) Clauses.

{*Success* | *That we should succeed in this plan*} is improbable.

The thought in these two sentences is the same, but in the second it is more fully expressed. In the first sentence, the subject is the noun *success*; in the second, the subject is the noun clause, *that we should succeed in this plan.* This clause is introduced by the conjunction *that*; the simple subject of the clause is the pronoun *we,* and the simple predicate is the verb-phrase *should succeed.* The first sentence is **simple**; the second is **complex**.

Substantive clauses are often introduced by the conjunction *that.*

49. II. Adjective Clauses. The following sentences illustrate the use of (1) an **adjective**, (2) an **adjective phrase**, (3) an **adjective clause**, as a modifier of the subject noun.

{An *honorable* man | A man *of honor* | A man *who values his honor*} will not lie.

{A *seasonable* word | A word *in season* | A word *that is spoken at the right moment*} may save a soul.

{My *native* land | The land *of my birth* | The land *where I was born*} lies far across the sea.

The first two sentences in each group are **simple**, the third is **complex**.

50. III. ADVERBIAL CLAUSES. The following sentences illustrate the use of (1) an **adverb**, (2) an **adverbial phrase**, (3) an **adverbial clause**, as a modifier of the predicate verb (or verb-phrase).

The lightning struck {*here. | on this spot. | where we stand.*}

Mr. Andrews lives {*near. | in this neighborhood. | where you see that elm.*}

The game began {*punctually. | on the stroke of one. | when the clock struck.*}

The banker will make the loan {*conditionally. | on one condition. | if you endorse my note.*}

The first two sentences in each group are **simple**, the third is **complex**.

51. Adjective clauses may be introduced (1) by the pronouns *who, which,* and *that,* or (2) by adverbs like *where, whence, whither, when.*

Adverbial clauses may be introduced (1) by the adverbs *where, whither, whence, when, while, before, after, until, how, as,* or (2) by the conjunctions *because, though, although, if, that* (*in order that, so that*), *lest,* etc.

> NOTE. The use of **phrases** and **clauses** as **parts of speech** increases enormously the richness and power of language. Though English has a huge stock of words, it cannot provide a separate noun or adjective or adverb for every idea. By grouping words, however, in phrases and clauses we, in effect, make a great variety of new nouns, adjectives, and adverbs, each precisely fitted to the needs of the moment in the expression of thought.

SUMMARY OF DEFINITIONS

THE SENTENCE

1. Language is thought expressed in words.

2. To express thought words are combined into sentences.

3. A sentence is a group of words which expresses a complete thought.

4. Sentences may be declarative, interrogative, imperative, or exclamatory.

(1) A declarative sentence declares or asserts something as a fact.

(2) An interrogative sentence asks a question.

(3) An imperative sentence expresses a command or a request.

(4) An exclamatory sentence expresses surprise, grief, or some other emotion in the form of an exclamation or cry.

A declarative, an interrogative, or an imperative sentence may also be exclamatory.

SUBJECT AND PREDICATE

5. Every sentence consists of a subject and a predicate.

The subject of a sentence designates the person, place, or thing that is spoken of; the predicate is that which is said of the subject.

6. The simple subject of a sentence is a noun or pronoun.

The simple predicate of a sentence is a verb or verb-phrase.

7. The simple subject, with such words as explain or complete its meaning, forms the complete subject.

The simple predicate, with such words as explain or complete its meaning, forms the complete predicate.

8. A compound subject or predicate consists of two or more simple subjects or predicates, joined, when necessary, by conjunctions.

Either the subject or the predicate, or both, may be compound.

THE PARTS OF SPEECH

9. In accordance with their use in the sentence, words are divided into eight classes called parts of speech,—namely, nouns, pronouns, adjectives, verbs, adverbs, prepositions, conjunctions, and interjections.

(1) A noun is the name of a person, place, or thing.

(2) A pronoun is a word used instead of a noun. It designates a person, place, or thing without naming it.

Nouns and pronouns are called substantives.

The substantive to which a pronoun refers is called its antecedent.

(3) An adjective is a word which describes or limits a substantive.

This it usually does by indicating some quality.

An adjective is said to belong to the substantive which it describes or limits.

An adjective which describes is called a descriptive adjective; one which points out or designates is called a definitive adjective.

(4) A verb is a word which can assert something (usually an action) concerning a person, place, or thing.

Some verbs express state or condition rather than action.

A group of words that is used as a verb is called a verb-phrase.

Certain verbs, when used to make verb-phrases, are called auxiliary (that is, "aiding") verbs, because they help other verbs to express action or state of some particular kind.

Is (in its various forms) and several other verbs may be used to frame sentences in which some word or words in the predicate describe or define the subject. In such sentences, *is* and other verbs that are used for the same purpose are called copulative (that is, "joining") verbs.

(5) An adverb is a word which modifies a verb, an adjective, or another adverb.

A word or group of words that changes or modifies the meaning of another word is called a modifier.

Adjectives and adverbs are both modifiers.

(6) A preposition is a word placed before a substantive to show its relation to some other word in the sentence.

The substantive which follows a preposition is called its object.

(7) A conjunction connects words or groups of words.

(8) An interjection is a cry or other exclamatory sound expressing surprise, anger, pleasure, or some other emotion or feeling.

10. The meaning of a word in the sentence determines to what part of speech it belongs.

The same word may be sometimes one part of speech, sometimes another.

11. The infinitive is a verb-form which partakes of the nature of a noun. It is commonly preceded by the preposition *to*, which is called the sign of the infinitive.

12. The participle is a verb-form which has no subject, but which partakes of the nature of an adjective and expresses action or state in such a way as to describe or limit a substantive.

A participle is said to belong to the substantive which it describes or limits.

The chief classes of participles are present participles and past participles, so called from the time which they denote.

SUBSTITUTES FOR THE PARTS OF SPEECH

PHRASES

13. A group of connected words, not containing a subject and a predicate, is called a phrase.

A phrase is often equivalent to a part of speech.

(1) A phrase used as a noun is called a noun-phrase.

(2) A phrase used as a verb is called a verb-phrase.

(3) A phrase used as an adjective is called an adjective phrase.

(4) A phrase used as an adverb is called an adverbial phrase.

14. Adjective or adverbial phrases consisting of a preposition and its object, with or without other words, may be called prepositional phrases.

Clauses

15. A clause is a group of words that forms part of a sentence and that contains a subject and a predicate.

16. A clause used as a part of speech is called a subordinate clause. All other clauses are said to be independent.

17. Clauses of the same order or rank are said to be coördinate.

18. Sentences may be simple, compound, or complex.

(1) A simple sentence has but one subject and one predicate, either or both of which may be compound.

(2) A compound sentence consists of two or more independent coördinate clauses, which may or may not be joined by conjunctions.

(3) A complex sentence consists of two or more clauses, one of which is independent and the rest subordinate.

A compound sentence in which one or more of the coördinate clauses are complex is called a compound complex sentence.

19. Subordinate clauses, like phrases, are used as parts of speech. They serve as substitutes for nouns, for adjectives, or for adverbs.

(1) A subordinate clause that is used as a noun is called a noun (or substantive) clause.

(2) A subordinate clause that modifies a substantive is called an adjective clause.

(3) A subordinate clause that serves as an adverbial modifier is called an adverbial clause.

PART TWO
INFLECTION AND SYNTAX

CHAPTER I
INFLECTION

52. Inflection is a change of form in a word indicating some change in its meaning. A word thus changed in form is said to be inflected.

Thus the nouns *man, wife, dog,* may change their form to *man's, wife's, dog's,* to express possession; or to *men, wives, dogs,* to show that two or more are meant.

The pronouns *I, she,* may change their form to *our, her.*

The adjectives *large, happy, good,* may change their form to *larger, happier, better,* to denote a higher degree of the quality; or to *largest, happiest, best,* to denote the highest degree.

The verbs *look, see, sing,* may change their form to *looked, saw, sang,* to denote past time.

The examples show that a word may be inflected (1) by the addition of a final letter or syllable (*dog, dogs*; *look, looked*), (2) by the substitution of one letter for another (*man, men*), or (3) by a complete change of form (*good, better, best*).

53. The inflection of a substantive is called its **declension**; that of an adjective or an adverb, its **comparison**; that of a verb, its **conjugation**.

NOTE. Some forms which we regard as due to inflection are really distinct words. Thus *we* is regarded as a form of the pronoun *I,* but it is in fact an altogether different word. Such irregularities, however, are not numerous, and are properly enough included under the head of inflection.

The table below gives a summary view of inflection, and may be used for reference with the following chapters.

Substantives (Nouns and Pronouns)

Gender

> Masculine (*male*)
>
> Feminine (*female*)
>
> Neuter (*no sex*)

Number

> Singular (*one*)
>
> Plural (*more than one*)

Person

> First (*speaker*)
>
> Second (*spoken to*)
>
> Third (*spoken of*)

Case

> Nominative (*subject case*)
>
> Possessive (*ownership*)
>
> Objective (*object case*)

Adjectives and Adverbs

Comparison

> Positive Degree
>
> Comparative Degree
>
> Superlative Degree

Verbs

Number (*Verb agrees with Subject*)

> Singular
>
> Plural

Person (*Verb agrees with Subject*)

> First

Second

Third

Tense

    Simple Tenses

        Present

        Past

        Future

    Compound Tenses

        Perfect (or Present Perfect)

        Pluperfect (or Past Perfect)

        Future Perfect

Mood

    Indicative (*all six tenses*)

    Imperative (*Present Tense only*)

    Subjunctive (*Present, Past, Perfect, Pluperfect*)

Voice

    Active (*Subject acts*)

    Passive (*Subject receives the action*)

Infinitives (Present and Perfect)

Participles (Present, Past, and Perfect)

CHAPTER II
NOUNS

CLASSIFICATION—COMMON NOUNS AND PROPER NOUNS

54. A noun is the name of a person, place, or thing.

55. Nouns are divided into two classes—proper nouns and common nouns.

1. **A proper noun is the name of a particular person, place, or thing.**

EXAMPLES: Lincoln, Napoleon, Ruth, Gladstone, America, Denver, Jove, Ohio, Monday, December, Yale, Christmas, Britannia, Niagara, Merrimac, Elmwood, Louvre, Richardson, Huron, Falstaff.

2. **A common noun is a name which may be applied to any one of a class of persons, places, or things.**

EXAMPLES: general, emperor, president, clerk, street, town, desk, tree, cloud, chimney, childhood, idea, thought, letter, dynamo, cruiser, dictionary, railroad.

Proper nouns begin with a capital letter; common nouns usually begin with a small letter.

NOTE. Although a proper noun is the name of a particular person, place, or thing, that name may be given to more than one individual. More than one man is named *James*; but when we say *James*, we think of one particular person, whom we are calling by his own name. When we say *man*, on the contrary, we are not calling any single person by name: we are using a noun which applies, in common, to all the members of a large class of persons.

Any word, when mentioned merely **as a word**, is a noun. Thus,—

And is a conjunction.

56. A common noun becomes a proper noun when used as the particular name of a ship, a newspaper, an animal, etc.

Nelson's flagship was the *Victory*.
Give me this evening's *Herald*.
My dog is named *Rover*.
The *Limited Express* is drawn by the *Pioneer*.

57. A proper noun often consists of a group of words, some of which are perhaps ordinarily used as other parts of speech.

EXAMPLES: James Russell Lowell, Washington Elm, Eiffel Tower, Firth of Clyde, North Lexington Junction, Stony Brook, Westminster Abbey, Measure for Measure, White House, Brooklyn Bridge, Atlantic Railroad, Sherman Act, The Return of the Native, Flatiron Building.

NOTE. These are (strictly speaking) noun-phrases (§ 41); but, since all are particular names, they may be regarded as proper nouns.

58. A proper noun becomes a common noun when used as a name that may be applied to any one of a class of objects.

The museum owns two *Rembrandts* and a *Titian*.
I exchanged my old motor car for a new *Halstead*.
My fountain pen is a *Blake*.
Lend me your *Webster*.
He was a *Napoleon* of finance.
I am going to buy a *Kazak*.

59. Certain proper nouns have become common nouns when used in a special sense. These generally begin with a small letter.

EXAMPLES: macadam (crushed stone for roads, so called from Macadam, the inventor), mackintosh (a waterproof garment), napoleon (a coin), guinea (twenty-one shillings), mentor (a wise counsellor), derringer (a kind of pistol).

60. A lifeless object, one of the lower animals, or any human quality or emotion is sometimes regarded as a person.

This usage is called **personification**, and the object, animal, or quality is said to be **personified**.

> Each old poetic *Mountain*
> Inspiration breathed around.—GRAY.

> Who'll toll the bell?
> "I," said the *Bull,*
> "Because I can pull."

> His name was *Patience.*—SPENSER.

> Smiles on past *Misfortune's* brow
> Soft *Reflection's* hand can trace;
> And o'er the cheek of *Sorrow* throw
>   A melancholy grace.—GRAY.

> *Love* is and was my lord and king,
>   And in his presence I attend.—TENNYSON.

> *Time* gently shakes his wings.—DRYDEN.

The name of anything personified is regarded as a proper noun and is usually written with a capital letter.

NOTE. The rule for capitals is not absolute. When the personification is kept up for only a sentence or two (as frequently in Shakspere), the noun often begins with a small letter.

SPECIAL CLASSES OF NOUNS

61. An abstract noun is the name of a quality or general idea.

EXAMPLES: blackness, freshness, smoothness, weight, height, length, depth, strength, health, honesty, beauty, liberty, eternity, satisfaction, precision, splendor, terror, disappointment, elegance, existence, grace, peace.

Many abstract nouns are derived from adjectives.

EXAMPLES: greenness (from *green*), depth (from *deep*), freedom (from *free*), wisdom (from *wise*), rotundity (from *rotund*), falsity or falseness (from *false*), bravery (from *brave*).

62. A collective noun is the name of a group, class, or multitude, and not of a single person, place, or thing.

EXAMPLES: crowd, group, legislature, squadron, sheaf, battalion, squad, Associated Press, Mediterranean Steamship Company, Senior Class, School Board.

The same noun may be **abstract** in one of its meanings, **collective** in another.

> They believe in *fraternity*. [Abstract.]
> The student joined a *fraternity*. [Collective.]

63. Abstract nouns are usually common, but become proper when the quality or idea is personified (§ 60).

Collective nouns may be either proper or common.

64. A noun consisting of two or more words united is called a compound noun.

EXAMPLES: (1) common nouns,— tablecloth, sidewalk, lampshade, bedclothes, steamboat, fireman, washerwoman, jackknife, hatband, headache, flatiron, innkeeper, knife-edge, steeple-climber, brother-in-law, commander-in-chief, window curtain, insurance company; (2) proper nouns,— Johnson, Williamson, Cooperstown, Louisville, Holywood, Elk-horn, Auburndale, Stratford-on-Avon, Lowell Junction.

As the examples show, the parts of a compound noun may be joined (with or without a hyphen) or written separately. In some words usage is fixed, in others it varies. The hyphen, however, is less used than formerly.

NOTE. The first part of a compound noun usually limits the second after the manner of an adjective. Indeed, many expressions may be regarded either (1) as compounds or (2) as phrases containing an adjective and a noun. Thus *railway conductor* may be taken as a compound noun, or as a noun (*conductor*) limited by an adjective (*railway*).

INFLECTION OF NOUNS

65. In studying the inflection of nouns and pronouns we have to consider **gender**, **number**, **person**, and **case**.

1. **Gender is distinction according to sex.**

2. **Number is that property of substantives which shows whether they indicate one person or thing or more than one.**

3. **Person is that property of substantives which shows whether they designate (1) the speaker, (2) the person spoken to, or (3) the person or thing spoken of.**

4. **Substantives have inflections of case to indicate their grammatical relations to verbs, to prepositions, or to other substantives.**

These four properties of substantives are included under inflection for convenience. In strictness, however, nouns are inflected for number and case only. Gender is shown in various ways,—usually by the meaning of the noun or by the use of some pronoun. Person is indicated by the sense, by the pronouns used, and by the form of the verb.

I. GENDER

66. Gender is distinction according to sex.

Nouns and pronouns may be of the masculine, the feminine, or the neuter gender.

1. **A noun or pronoun denoting a male being is of the masculine gender.**

> EXAMPLES: Joseph, boy, cockerel, buck, footman, butler, brother, father, uncle, he.

2. **A noun or pronoun denoting a female being is of the feminine gender.**

> EXAMPLES: girl, Julia, hen, waitress, maid, doe, spinster, matron, aunt, squaw, she.

3. **A noun or pronoun denoting a thing without animal life is of the neuter gender.**

> EXAMPLES: pencil, light, water, star, book, dust, leaf, it.

A noun or pronoun which is sometimes masculine and sometimes feminine is often said to be of **common gender**.

> EXAMPLES: bird, speaker, artist, animal, cat, European, musician, operator, they.

67. A pronoun must be in the same gender as the noun for which it stands or to which it refers.

Each of the following pronouns is limited to a single gender:

MASCULINE: *he, his, him.*
FEMININE: *she, her, hers.*
NEUTER: *it, its.*

All other pronouns vary in gender.

> *Robert* greeted *his* employer. [Masculine.]
> A *mother* passed with *her* child. [Feminine.]
> This *tree* has lost *its* foliage. [Neuter.]
> *Who* laughed? [Masculine or feminine.]
> How do *you* do? [Masculine or feminine.]
> *They* have disappeared. [Masculine, feminine, or neuter.]
> I do not care for *either*. [Masculine, feminine, or neuter.]

68. A neuter noun may become masculine or feminine by **personification** (§ 60).

> Thou who didst waken from his summer dreams
> The blue Mediterranean.—SHELLEY.

> Stern daughter of the Voice of God!
> O Duty!—WORDSWORTH.

>   Nature from her seat
> Sighing through all her works, gave signs of woe.—MILTON.

69. In speaking of certain objects, such as a ship and the moon, it is customary to use *she* and *her*. In like manner, *he* is used in speaking of the sun and of most animals, without reference to sex, although *it* often designates an insect or other small creature, and even a very young child.

Who and *which* are both used in referring to the **lower animals**. *Which* is the commoner, but *who* is not infrequent, especially if the animal is thought of as an intelligent being.

Thus one would say, "The dog *which* is for sale is in that kennel," even if one added, "*He* is a collie." But *which* would never be used in such a sentence as, "I have a dog *who* loves children."

70. The **gender** of masculine and of feminine nouns may be shown in various ways.

1. The male and the female of many kinds or classes of living beings are denoted by different words.

MASCULINE	FEMININE
father	mother
husband	wife
uncle	aunt
king	queen
monk	nun
wizard	witch
lord	lady
horse	mare
gander	goose
drake	duck
cock	hen
ram	ewe
bull	cow
hart	hind
buck	doe
fox	vixen[10]

2. Some masculine nouns become feminine by the addition of an ending.

MASCULINE	FEMININE

heir	heiress
baron	baroness
lion	lioness
prince	princess
emperor	empress
tiger	tigress
executor	executrix
administrator	administratrix
hero	heroine
Joseph	Josephine
sultan	sultana
Philip	Philippa

NOTE. The feminine gender is often indicated by the ending *ess*. Frequently the corresponding masculine form ends in *or* or *er*: as,—actor, actress; governor, governess; waiter, waitress. The ending *ess* is not so common as formerly. Usage favors *proprietor, author, editor,* etc., even for the feminine (rather than the harsher forms *proprietress, authoress, editress*), whenever there is no special reason for emphasizing the difference of sex.

3. A few feminine words become masculine by the addition of an ending. Thus,—*widow, widower; bride, bridegroom.*

4. Gender is sometimes indicated by the ending *man, woman, maid, boy,* or *girl.*

EXAMPLES: salesman, saleswoman; foreman, forewoman; laundryman; milkmaid; cash boy, cash girl.

5. A noun or a pronoun is sometimes prefixed to a noun to indicate gender.

EXAMPLES: manservant, maidservant; mother bird; cock sparrow, hen sparrow; boy friend, girl friend; he-wolf, she-wolf.

6. The gender of a noun may be indicated by some accompanying part of speech, usually by a pronoun.

> My *cat* is always washing *his* face.
>
> The *intruder* shook *her* head.
>
> I was confronted by a pitiful *creature*, haggard and *unshaven*.

NOTE. The variations in form studied under 2 and 3 (above) are often regarded as inflections. In reality, however, the masculine and the feminine are different words. Thus, *baroness* is not an inflectional form of *baron*, but a distinct noun, made from *baron* by adding the ending *ess*, precisely as *barony* and *baronage* are made from *baron* by adding the endings *y* and *age*. The process is rather that of **derivation** or noun-formation than that of inflection.

II. NUMBER

71. Number is that property of substantives which shows whether they indicate one person, place, or thing or more than one.

There are two numbers,—the singular and the plural.

The singular number denotes but one person, place, or thing. The plural number denotes more than one person, place, or thing.

72. Most nouns form the plural number by adding *s* or *es* to the singular.

> EXAMPLES: mat, mats; wave, waves; problem, problems; bough, boughs; John, Johns; nurse, nurses; tense, tenses; bench, benches; dish, dishes; class, classes; fox, foxes.

SPECIAL RULES

1. If the singular ends in *s, x, z, ch,* or *sh,* the plural ending is *es.*

> EXAMPLES: loss, losses; box, boxes; buzz, buzzes; match, matches; rush, rushes.

2. Many nouns ending in *o* preceded by a consonant also take the ending *es* in the plural.

    Examples: hero, heroes; cargo, cargoes; potato, potatoes; motto, mottoes; buffalo, buffaloes; mosquito, mosquitoes.

3. Nouns ending in *o* preceded by a vowel form their plural in *s*: as,— *cameo, cameos*; *folio, folios*.

4. The following nouns ending in *o* preceded by a consonant also form their plural in *s*:—

    banjo
    bravo
    burro
    cantocasino
    chromo
    contralto
    duodecimo
    dynamo
    halo[11]
    junto
    lasso
    memento[11]
    octavo
    piano
    proviso
    quarto
    solo
    soprano
    stiletto
    torso

tyro

zero[11]

73. In some nouns the addition of the plural ending alters the spelling and even the sound of the singular form.

1. Nouns ending in *y* preceded by a consonant change *y* to *i* and add *es* in the plural.

> EXAMPLES: sky, skies; fly, flies; country, countries; berry, berries. (Contrast: valley, valleys; chimney, chimneys; monkey, monkeys; boy, boys; day, days.)

Most proper names ending in *y*, however, take the plural in *s*.

> EXAMPLES: Mary, Marys; Murphy, Murphys; Daly, Dalys; Rowley, Rowleys; May, Mays.

2. Some nouns ending in *f* or *fe*, change the *f* to *v* and add *es* or *s*.

> EXAMPLES: wharf, wharves; wife, wives; shelf, shelves; wolf, wolves; thief, thieves; knife, knives; half, halves; calf, calves; life, lives; self, selves; sheaf, sheaves; loaf, loaves; leaf, leaves; elf, elves; beef, beeves.

74. A few nouns form their plural in *en*.

> These are: ox, oxen; brother, brethren (*or* brothers); child, children.

> NOTE. Ancient or poetical plurals belonging to this class are: *eyne* (for *eyen*, from *eye*), *kine* (cows), *shoon* (shoes), *hosen* (hose).

75. A few nouns form their plural by a **change of vowel**.

> These are: man, men; woman, women; merman, mermen; foot, feet; tooth, teeth; goose, geese; mouse, mice; louse, lice. Also

compound words ending in *man* or *woman*, such as fireman, firemen; saleswoman, saleswomen; Dutchman, Dutchmen.

NOTE. *German, Mussulman, Ottoman, dragoman, firman,* and *talisman,* which are not compounds of *man,* form their plurals regularly: as,—*Germans, Mussulmans. Norman* also forms its plural in *s.*

76. A few nouns have the same form in both singular and plural.

EXAMPLES: deer, sheep, heathen, Japanese, Portuguese, Iroquois.

NOTE. This class was larger in older English than at present. It included, for example, *year,* which in Shakspere has two plurals:—"six thousand *years,*" "twelve *year* since."

77. A few nouns have two plurals, but usually with some difference in meaning.

SINGULAR	PLURAL
brother	brothers (relatives)
	brethren (members of the same society)
horse	horses (animals)
	horse (cavalry)
foot	feet (parts of the body)
	foot (infantry)
sail	sails (on vessels)
	sail (vessels in a fleet)
head	heads (in usual sense)
	head (of cattle)
fish	fishes (individually)
	fish (collectively)
penny	pennies (single coins)
	pence (collectively)
cloth	cloths (pieces of cloth)

	clothes (garments)
die	dies (for stamping)
	dice (for gaming)

The *pennies* were arranged in neat piles.

English money is reckoned in pounds, shillings, and *pence*.

78. When **compound nouns** are made plural, the last part usually takes the plural form; less often the first part; rarely both parts.

EXAMPLES: spoonful, spoonfuls; bathhouse, bathhouses; forget-me-not, forget-me-nots; editor-in-chief, editors-in-chief; maid-of-honor, maids-of-honor; gentleman usher, gentlemen ushers; Knight Templar, Knights Templars; Lord Justice, Lords Justices; manservant, menservants.

79. Letters of the alphabet, figures, signs used in writing, and words regarded merely as words take 's in the plural.

"Embarrassed" is spelled with two *r*'s and two *s*'s.

Your *3*'s look like *8*'s.

Tell the printer to change the §'s to ¶'s.

Don't interrupt me with your *but*'s!

80. Foreign nouns in English sometimes retain their foreign plurals; but many have an English plural also.

Some of the commonest are included in the following list:[12]

SINGULAR	PLURAL
alumna (feminine)	alumnæ
alumnus (masculine)	alumni
amanuensis	amanuenses

analysis	analyses
animalculum	animalcula[13]
antithesis	antitheses
appendix	appendices
	appendixes
axis	axes
bacillus	bacilli
bacterium	bacteria
bandit	banditti
	bandits
basis	bases
beau	beaux
	beaus
candelabrum	candelabra
cumulus	cumuli
cherub	cherubim
	cherubs
crisis	crises
curriculum	curricula
datum	data
ellipsis	ellipses
erratum	errata
formula	formulæ
	formulas
genius	genii
	geniuses
genus	genera
gymnasium	gymnasia

	gymnasiums
hippopotamus	hippopotami
hypothesis	hypotheses
larva	larvæ
memorandum	memoranda
	memorandums
nebula	nebulæ
oasis	oases
parenthesis	parentheses
phenomenon	phenomena
radius	radii
seraph	seraphim
	seraphs
species	species
stratum	strata
synopsis	synopses
tableau	tableaux
tempo	tempi
terminus	termini
thesis	theses
trousseau	trousseaux
vertebra	vertebræ

The two plurals sometimes differ in meaning: as,—

Michael Angelo and Raphael were *geniuses*.
Spirits are sometimes called *genii*.
This book has two *indices*.
The printer uses signs called *indexes*.

81. When a **proper name** with the title *Mr., Mrs., Miss,* or *Master,* is put into the plural, the rules are as follows:—

1. The plural of *Mr.* is *Messrs.* (pronounced *Messers*[14]). The name remains in the singular. Thus,—

> *Mr. Jackson,* plural *Messrs.* (or the *Messrs.*) *Jackson.*

2. *Mrs.* has no plural. The name itself takes the plural form. Thus,—

> *Mrs. Jackson,* plural *the Mrs. Jacksons.*

3. In the case of *Miss,* sometimes the title is put into the plural, sometimes the name. Thus,—

> *Miss Jackson,* plural *the Misses Jackson* or *the Miss Jacksons.*

> The latter expression is somewhat informal. Accordingly, it would not be used in a formal invitation or reply, or in addressing a letter.

4. The plural of *Master* is *Masters.* The name remains in the singular. Thus,—

> *Master Jackson,* plural *the Masters Jackson.*

> Other titles usually remain in the singular, the name taking the plural form: as,—*the two General Follansbys.* But when two or more names follow, the title becomes plural: as,— *Generals Rolfe and Johnson.*

82. Some nouns, on account of their meaning, are seldom or never used in the plural.

> Such are many names of qualities (as *cheerfulness, mirth*), of sciences (as *chemistry*[15]), of forces (as *gravitation*).

Many nouns, commonly used in the singular only, may take a plural in some special sense. Thus,—

earth (the globe)	earths (kinds of soil)
ice (frozen water)	ices (food)
tin (a metal)	tins (tin dishes or cans)
nickel (a metal)	nickels (coins)

83. Some nouns are used in the plural only.

Such are: annals, athletics, billiards, dregs, eaves, entrails, lees, nuptials, oats, obsequies, pincers, proceeds, riches, scissors, shears, suds, tweezers, tongs, trousers, victuals, vitals; and (in certain special senses) ashes, goods, links, scales, spectacles, stocks.

84. A few nouns are plural in form, but singular in meaning.

Such are: gallows, news, measles, mumps, small pox (for *small pocks*), politics, and some names of sciences (as, civics, economics, ethics, mathematics, physics, optics).

NOTE. These nouns were formerly plural in sense as well as in form. *News*, for example, originally meant "new things." Shakspere uses it both as a singular and as a plural. Thus, —"*This news* was brought to Richard" (*King John*, v. 3. 12); "But wherefore do I tell *these news* to thee?" (*1 Henry IV*, iii. 2. 121). In a few words modern usage varies. The following nouns are sometimes singular, sometimes plural: *alms, amends, bellows, means, pains* (in the sense of "effort"), *tidings*.

III. PERSON

85. Person is that property of substantives which shows whether they denote (1) the speaker, (2) the person spoken to, or (3) the person spoken of.

A substantive is in the first person when it denotes the speaker, in the second person when it denotes the person spoken to, in the third person when it denotes the person or thing spoken of.

I, the *king*, command his presence. [First person.]

You, *Thomas*, broke the window. [Second person.]

Charles, come here. [Second person.]

He, the *fireman*, saved the train. [Third person.]

The *diver* sinks slowly from our view. [Third person.]

The *tower* suddenly collapsed. [Third person.]

The examples show (1) that the person of a noun has nothing to do with its form, but is indicated by the sense or connection; (2) that certain pronouns denote person with precision. Thus, *I* is always of the first person; *you* of the second; and *he* of the third. These personal pronouns will be treated in Chapter III.

IV. CASE

86. Substantives have inflections of case to indicate their grammatical relations to verbs, to prepositions, or to other substantives.

There are three cases,—the **nominative**, the **possessive**, and the **objective**.

The possessive case is often called the **genitive**.

The nominative and the objective case of a noun are always alike in form. In some pronouns, however, there is a difference (as,—*I, me; he, him*).

DECLENSION OF NOUNS

87. The inflection of a substantive is called its **declension**. To **decline** a noun is to give its case-forms in order, first in the singular number and then in the plural. Thus,—

SINGULAR							
Nominative	boy	horse	fly	chimney	calf	lass	man	deer

Possessive	boy's	horse's	fly's	chimney's	calf's	lass's	man's	deer's
Objective	boy	horse	fly	chimney	calf	lass	man	deer
PLURAL								
Nominative	boys	horses	flies	chimneys	calves	lasses	men	deer
Possessive	boys'	horses'	flies'	chimneys'	calves'	lasses'	men's	deer's
Objective	boys	horses	flies	chimneys	calves	lasses	men	deer

NOMINATIVE CASE

88. The **nominative case** is used in the following constructions: (1) the subject, (2) the predicate nominative, (3) the vocative, (or nominative of direct address), (4) the exclamatory nominative, (5) appositive with a nominative, (6) the nominative absolute.

1. **The subject of a verb is in the nominative case.**

> *Water* freezes.
> *Charles* climbed the mountain.
> The boy's *face* glowed with health and exercise.
> A thousand *men* were killed in this battle.

In the third example, *face* is the simple subject; the complete subject is *the boy's face*. In the fourth, *men* is the simple subject; the complete subject is *a thousand men*. Both *face* and *men* are in the nominative case; *face* is in the singular number; *men* in the plural.

2. **A substantive standing in the predicate, but describing or defining the subject, agrees with the subject in case and is called a predicate nominative.**

> A predicate nominative is also called a **subject complement** or an **attribute**.

> Lobsters are *crustaceans*.
> A good book is a faithful *friend*.

Shakspere was a *native* of Stratford-on-Avon.

Arnold proved a *traitor.*

Adams was elected *president.*

The rule for the case of the predicate nominative is particularly important with respect to pronouns (§ 119).

| I am *he.* | Are you *she*? |
| It is *I.* | It was *we* who did it. |

The predicate nominative is commonest after the copula *is* (in its various forms). It will be further studied in connection with intransitive and passive verbs (§§ 214, 252).

3. **A substantive used for the purpose of addressing a person directly, and not connected with any verb, is called a vocative.**

A vocative is in the nominative case, and is often called a **nominative by direct address** or a **vocative nominative**.

Come, *Ruth,* give me your hand.

Turn to the right, *madam.*

Herbert, it is your turn.

Come with me, my *child.*

NOTE. A vocative word is sometimes said to be **independent by direct address**, because it stands by itself, unconnected with any verb. That a vocative is really in the nominative case may be seen in the use of the pronoun *thou* in this construction: as,—I will arrest thee, *thou* traitor (see § 115).

4. **A substantive used as an exclamation is called an exclamatory nominative (or nominative of exclamation).**

Peace, be still.

Fortunate *Ruth*!

A *drum*! a *drum*! Macbeth doth come.

Look! a *balloon*!

The *sun*! then we shall have a fine day.

Certain exclamatory nominatives are sometimes classed as interjections (§ 375).

5. **A substantive added to another substantive to explain it and signifying the same person or thing, is called an appositive and is said to be in apposition.**

An appositive is in the same case as the substantive which it limits.

Hence a substantive in apposition with a nominative is in the nominative case.

Mr. Scott, the *grocer*, is here. [Apposition with subject.]

Tom, old *fellow*, I am glad to see you. [Apposition with vocative.]

The discoverer of the Pacific was Balboa, a *Spaniard*. [Apposition with predicate nominative.]

NOTE. *Apposition* means "attachment"; *appositive* means "attached noun or pronoun." An appositive modifies the noun with which it is in apposition much as an adjective might do (compare "Balboa, a *Spaniard*" with "*Spanish* Balboa"). Hence it is classed as an adjective modifier.

POSSESSIVE CASE

89. **The possessive case denotes ownership or possession.**

John's yacht lies at her moorings.

The *duck's* feet are webbed.

The *mutineer's* pistol burst when he fired.

NOTE. Most uses of the possessive come under the general head of **possession** in some sense. Special varieties of meaning are **source** (as in "*hen's* eggs") and **authorship** (as in "*Wordsworth's* sonnets").

A possessive noun or pronoun modifies the substantive to which it is attached as an adjective might do. Hence it is classed as an adjective modifier.

Forms of the Possessive Case

90. The possessive case of most nouns has, in the singular number, the ending *'s*.

EXAMPLES: the owl's feathers, Elizabeth's hat, the officer's name.

Plural nouns ending in *s* take no further ending for the possessive. In writing, however, an apostrophe is put after the *s* to indicate the possessive case.

EXAMPLES: the owls' feathers, the officers' names, the artists' petition, the engineers' ball.

Plural nouns not ending in *s* take *'s* in the possessive.

EXAMPLES: the firemen's ball, the policemen's quarters, the children's hour.

NOTE. In older English the possessive of most nouns was written as well as pronounced with the ending *-es* or *-is*. Thus, in Chaucer, the possessive of *child* is *childës* or *childis*; that of *king* is *kingës* or *kingis*; that of *John* is *Johnës* or *Johnis*. The use of an apostrophe in the possessive is a comparatively modern device, due to a misunderstanding. Scholars at one time thought the *s* of the possessive a fragment of the pronoun *his*; that is, they took such a phrase as *George's book* for a contraction of *George his book*. Hence they used the apostrophe before *s* to signify the supposed omission of part of the word *his*. Similarly, in the possessive plural, there was thought to be an omission of a final *es*; that is, such a phrase as *the horses' heads* was thought to be a contraction of the *horseses* heads. Both these errors have long been exploded.

91. Nouns like *sheep* and *deer*, which have the same form in both the singular and the plural, usually take *'s* in the possessive plural.

Thus, *the deer's tracks* would be written, whether one deer or more were meant.

92. POSSESSIVE SINGULAR OF NOUNS ENDING IN *S*.

1. Monosyllabic nouns ending in *s* or an *s*-sound usually make their possessive singular by adding 's.

> EXAMPLES: Charles's hat, Forbes's garden, Mr. Wells's daughter, Rice's carriage, Mrs. Dix's family, a fox's brush.

> NOTE. Most of these monosyllabic nouns in s are family names. The rule accords with the best usage; but it is not absolute, for usage varies. Hence forms like *Charles'* and *Wells'* cannot be condemned as positively wrong, though *Charles's* and *Wells's* are preferable. In speaking, the shorter form is often ambiguous, for there is no difference in sound between *Dix'* and *Dick's, Mr. Hills'* and *Mr. Hill's, Dr. Childs'* and *Dr. Child's*.

2. Nouns of two or more syllables ending in *s* or an *s*-sound, and not accented on the last syllable, may make their possessive singular by adding 's, or may take no ending in the possessive.

In the latter case, an apostrophe is added in writing, but in sound there is no difference between the possessive and the nominative.

> EXAMPLES: Burrows's (*or* Burrows') Hotel, Æneas's (*or* Æneas') voyage, Beatrice's (*or* Beatrice') gratitude, Felix's (*or* Felix') arrival, for conscience's (*or* conscience') sake.

Most of the nouns in question are proper names. In speaking, one must often use the longer form to prevent ambiguity; for *Williams'* and *William's, Roberts'* and *Robert's, Robbins'* and *Robin's*, are indistinguishable in sound.

> NOTE. Nouns of two or more syllables ending in *s* or an *s*-sound and accented on the last syllable, follow the rule for monosyllables. Thus,—*Laplace's* mathematics (not *Laplace'*); *Alphonse's* father (not *Alphonse'*).
> When final *s* is silent (as in many French names), 's must of course be added in the possessive. Thus, —*Descartes's* philosophy (pronounced *Daycárt's*).

Use of the Possessive Case

93.[16] Possession may be denoted by a phrase with *of* as well as by the possessive case. The distinction between the two forms cannot be brought under rigid rules, but the following suggestions will be of use.

I. In older English and in poetry the possessive case of nouns is freely used, but in modern prose it is rare unless the possessor is a living being. A phrase with *of* is used instead.

> The mayor *of Detroit* (NOT *Detroit's* mayor).
> The top *of the post* (NOT the *post's* top).
> The prevalence *of the epidemic* (NOT the *epidemic's* prevalence).

Contrast the poetic use:—

> *Belgium's* capital had gathered then
> Her beauty and her chivalry.—BYRON.

Other prepositions are sometimes used: as,—"the explosion in *New York*" (NOT "*New York's* explosion"), "the station *at Plymouth.*"

II. When the possessor is a living being, good usage varies.

1. If there is actual ownership or possession of some material thing, the possessive case is generally used in the singular: as,—"John's *hat*" (not "the hat *of John*"). The possessive plural, however, is often replaced by a phrase with *of*, to avoid ambiguity or harshness: as,—"the jewels *of the ladies*" (rather than "the *ladies'* jewels")[17], "the wings *of the geese*" (rather than "the *geese's* wings").

2. With nouns denoting a quality, an act, or the like, either the possessive or the *of*-phrase is proper: as,—"*John's* generosity," or "the generosity *of John*"; "*John's* condition," or "the condition *of John*"; "the *guide's* efforts," or "the efforts *of the guide*"; "*Cæsar's* death," or "the death *of Cæsar.*"

When there is any choice, it usually depends on euphony (that is, agreeable sound), and is therefore a question of style. Sometimes, however, there is a distinction in sense. "*John's* fear," for example, indicates that John is afraid; but "the fear *of John*" means the fear which John inspires in others.

III. The following phrases are established idioms with the possessive. In some of them, however, the possessive may be replaced by *of* and its object.

> (1) The earth's surface, the sun's rays, the moon's reflection, the pit's mouth, a rope's end, his journey's end, at his wit's end, the ship's keel, the water's edge, the cannon's mouth, out of harm's way, at swords' points, for pity's sake, for conscience' sake; (2) a moment's

pause, a year's time, a hand's breadth, a boat's length, a month's salary, a week's notice, a night's rest, a day's work, a stone's throw, a feather's weight, an hour's delay, a dollar's worth, not a foot's difference.

In the second group of phrases ("a moment's pause," etc.), the possessive denotes not ownership, but **measure** or **extent**.

IV. The possessive case of certain pronouns (*my, our, your, his, her, its, their*) is more freely used than that of nouns in expressions that do not denote actual ownership.

I know him to *my* sorrow. [Compare: to his loss, to our detriment, to his advantage.]

The brass has lost *its* polish.

This question must be decided on *its* merits.

His arguments did not fail of *their* effect.

For the inflection of these pronouns, see § 115. For the use of *whose*, see § 152.

94. When a thing belongs to two or more **joint owners**, the sign of the possessive is added to the last name only.

Brown, Jones, and Richardson's factories. [Brown, Jones, and Richardson are partners.]

It is George and William's turn to take the boat. [George and William are to go in the boat together.]

On the other hand, in order to avoid ambiguity we should say, "Brown's, Jones's, and Richardson's factories," if each individual had a factory of his own; and "George's and William's answers were correct," if each boy answered independently of the other.

95. In **compound nouns** the last part takes the possessive sign. So also when a phrase is used as a noun.

My *father-in-law's* home is in Easton.

We had *a quarter of an hour's* talk.

Other examples are the following:—

My brother-in-law's opinion; the commander-in-chief's orders; the lady-in-waiting's duties; the coal dealer's prices; Edward VII's reign; the King of England's portrait; half a year's delay; in three or four months' time; a cable and a half's length; the pleasure of Major Pendennis and Mr. Arthur Pendennis's company (THACKERAY).

NOTE. Noun-phrases often contain two substantives, the second of which is in apposition with the first. In such phrases, *of* is generally preferable to the possessive. Thus, we may say either "Tom the blacksmith's daughter" or "the daughter of Tom the blacksmith"; but "the son of Mr. Hill the carpenter" is both neater and clearer than "Mr. Hill the carpenter's son." The use of *'s* is also avoided with a very long phrase like "the owner of the house on the other side of the street."

An objective may stand in apposition with a possessive, the latter being equivalent to *of* with an object. Thus,—"I am not yet of Percy's mind [= of the mind of Percy], the *Hotspur* of the North" (SHAKSPERE).

96. The noun denoting the object possessed is often omitted when it may be readily understood, especially in the predicate.

Conant's [shop] is open until noon.

I buy my hats at *Bryant's* [shop].

We will dine at *Pennock's* [restaurant].

That camera is *mine*. (See § 122.)

This construction is common in such expressions as:—

He was a relative of *John's*.

That careless tongue of *John's* will get him into trouble.

In the first example, "a relative of John's" means "a relative of (= *from among*) John's relatives." The second example shows an extension of this construction by analogy. See § 122.

97. The **objective case**, as its name implies, is the case of the **object**. Most of its uses are covered by the following rule:—

The object of a verb or preposition is in the objective case.

The object of a preposition has already been explained and defined (§§ 20–21).

98. The **object of a verb** may be (1) the direct object, (2) the predicate objective, (3) the indirect object, (4) the cognate object. Of these the direct object is the most important.

The objective is also used (5) adverbially (§ 109), (6) in apposition with another objective (§ 110), and (7) as the subject of an infinitive (§ 111).

1. Direct Object

99. Some verbs may be followed by a substantive denoting that which receives the action or is produced by it. These are called transitive verbs. All other verbs are called intransitive.

1. That man *struck* my *dog.*
2. The arrow *hit* the *target.*
3. Cæsar *conquered Gaul.*
4. Mr. Holland *sells flour.*
5. The farmer *raises corn.*
6. Mr. Eaton *makes stoves.*
7. My grandfather *built* that *house.*

In Nos. 1–4, the verb is followed by a noun denoting the **receiver of the action**. Thus, in the first sentence, the *dog* receives the blow; in the second, the *target* receives the action of hitting. In Nos. 5–7, the verb is followed by a noun denoting the **product** of the action. For example, the *corn* is **produced** by the action expressed by the verb *raises*.

In each example, the noun that follows the verb **completes the sense** of the verb. "That man *struck* ——." "Struck *whom*?" "He struck the *dog*." Until *dog* is added the sense of the verb *struck* is incomplete.

100. A substantive that completes the meaning of a transitive verb is called its direct object, and is said to be in the objective case.

Thus, in the examples above, *dog* is the direct object of the transitive verb *struck*; *target* is the direct object of *hit*,—and so on. Each of these nouns is therefore in the **objective case**.

The direct object is often called the object complement, or the object of the verb.

101. Intransitive verbs have no object.

> The lion *roared*.
> The visitor *coughed* gently.
> The log *drifted* downstream.
> We all *listened* intently.

Compare these sentences with those in § 99. We observe that the verbs (unlike those in § 99) admit no object, since their meaning is complete without the addition of any noun to denote the receiver or product of the action. "The man *struck*——" prompts the inquiry, "Struck *whom*?" But no such question is suggested by "The lion *roared*"; for "Roared *what*?" would be an absurdity.

102. The **predicate nominative** (§ 88, 2) must not be confused with the **direct object**. They resemble each other in two particulars: (1) both stand in the predicate, and (2) both complete the meaning of the verb. But they differ utterly in their relation to the subject of the sentence. For—

The **predicate nominative** describes or defines the **subject**. Hence both substantives denote the same person or thing.

> Charles [SUBJECT] {is | was | became | was elected} *captain* [PREDICATE NOMINATIVE].

The **direct object** neither describes nor defines the subject. On the contrary, it designates that upon which the subject acts. Hence the two substantives regularly[18] denote different persons or things.

> Charles [SUBJECT] {struck *James* [OBJECT]. | threw a *stone* [OBJECT]. | built a *boat* [OBJECT].}

Both the direct object and the predicate nominative are classed as **complements**, because they are used to complete the sense of the predicate verb (§ 483).

103. A verb of *asking* sometimes takes **two direct objects**, one denoting the **person** and the other the **thing**.

> She asked the *boy* his *name*.
> Ask *me* no *favors*.
> I asked the *lawyer* his *opinion*.

2. Predicate Objective

104. Verbs of *choosing, calling, naming, making,* and *thinking* may take two objects referring to the same person or thing.

The first of these is the direct object, and the second, which completes the sense of the predicate, is called a predicate objective.

> We chose Oscar *president*. [*Oscar* is the direct object of *chose*; *president* is the predicate objective.]
> I call John my *friend*.
> They thought the man a *coward*.
> Make my house your *home*.

The predicate objective is often called the complementary object or the objective attribute. It is classed as a complement.

An adjective may serve as predicate objective.

> I call this ship *unseaworthy*.
> Your letter made your sister *anxious*.
> What makes Edwin so *careless*?

3. Indirect Object and Similar Idioms

105. Some verbs of *giving, telling, refusing,* and the like, may take two objects, a direct object and an indirect object.

The indirect object denotes the person or thing toward whom or toward which is directed the action expressed by the rest of the predicate.

Direct Object only	Direct Object and Indirect Object
Dick sold his bicycle.	Dick sold *John* his bicycle.
I gave permission.	I gave this *man* permission.
He paid a dollar.	He paid the *gardener* a dollar.
She taught Latin.	She taught my *children* Latin.

Most of the verbs that admit an indirect object are included in the following list:—

> allot, allow, assign, bequeath, bring, deny, ensure, fetch, fling, forbid, forgive, give, grant, guarantee, hand, lease, leave, lend, let, owe, pardon, pass, pay, refund, refuse, remit, restore, sell, send, show, sing, spare, teach, tell, throw, toss, vouchsafe.

Pronouns are commoner as indirect objects than nouns.

> They denied *her* the necessities of life.
> I guaranteed *them* a handsome profit.
> The king vouchsafed *them* an audience.

It is always possible to insert the preposition *to* before the indirect object without changing the sense.

Since the indirect object is equivalent to an adverbial phrase, it is classed as a modifier of the verb.

> Thus, in "Dick sold *John* his bicycle," *John* is an adverbial modifier of the predicate verb *sold.*

The indirect object is sometimes used without a direct object expressed. Thus,—

> He paid the hatter.

> Here *hatter* may be recognized as an indirect object by inserting *to* before it and adding a direct object ("his *bill*," "his *money*," or the like).

106. The objective case sometimes expresses the person *for whom* anything is done.

> William made his *brother* a kite [= made a kite for his brother].
> Sampson built *me* a boat [= built a boat for me].

This construction may be called the **objective of service**.

> NOTE. The objective of service is often included under the head of the indirect object. But the two constructions differ widely in sense, and should be carefully distinguished. To do an act *to* a person is not the same thing as to do an act *for* a person. Contrast "John paid the money *to* me," with "John paid the money *for* me"; "Dick sold a bicycle *to* me," with "Dick sold a bicycle *for* me."

107. The objective case is used after *like, unlike, near,* and *next*, which are really adjectives or adverbs, though in this construction they are often regarded as prepositions.

> She sang like a *bird*. [*Like* is an adverb.]
> The earth is like a *ball*. [*Like* is an adjective.]
> My office is near the *station*. [*Near* is an adjective.]

That answer was unlike *Joseph*. [*Unlike* is an adjective.]

This man walks unlike *Joseph*. [*Unlike* is an adverb.]

A stream ran near the *hut*. [*Near* is an adverb.]

The use of the objective after these words is a peculiar idiom similar to the indirect object (§ 105). The nature of the construction may be seen (as in the indirect object) by inserting *to* or *unto* ("She sang *like unto* a bird").

NOTE. The indirect object, the objective of service, and the objective after *like*, *unlike*, and *near* are all survivals of old dative constructions. Besides the case of the direct object (often called **accusative**), English once had a case (called the **dative**) which meant *to* or *for* [somebody or something]. The dative case is easily distinguished in Greek, Latin, and German, but in English it has long been merged in form with the ordinary objective.

4. Cognate Object

108. A verb that is regularly intransitive sometimes takes as object a noun whose meaning closely resembles its own.

A noun in this construction is called the cognate object of the verb and is in the objective case.

He ran a *race*.

The mayor coughed a dubious, insinuating *cough*.

A scornful *laugh* laughed he.

The trumpeter blew a loud *blast*.

She sleeps the *sleep* of death.

NOTE. *Cognate* means "kindred" or "related." The cognate object repeats the idea of the verb, often with some modification, and may be classed as an adverbial modifier. Its difference from the direct object may be seen by contrasting "The blacksmith struck the *anvil*" with "The blacksmith struck a mighty *blow*" (cf. "struck *mightily*"). For the pronoun *it* as cognate object, see § 120.

5. Adverbial Objective

109. A noun, or a phrase consisting of a noun and its modifiers, may be used adverbially. Such a noun is called an adverbial objective.

> We have waited *years* for this reform.
> I am *years* older than you are.
> The river is *miles* away.
> The water rose *three feet*.
> This is *an inch* too long.
> My brother is *twenty years* old.
> I will stay a *short time*.
> Wait *a moment*.
> Come here *this instant*!
> Turn your eyes *this way*.
> This silk is *several shades* too light.

A group of words consisting of an adverbial object with its modifier or modifiers forms an **adverbial phrase** (§ 41).

6. Objective in Apposition

110. A substantive in apposition with an objective is itself in the objective case.

> Yesterday I saw Williams the *expressman*. [Apposition with the direct object of *saw*.]
> Tom gave his friend *John* a book. [Apposition with the indirect object *friend*.]
> He lives with Andrews the *blacksmith*. [Apposition with the object of the preposition *with*.]

This rule follows from the general principle that an appositive is in the same case as the substantive to which it is attached (§ 88, 5).

7. Subject of an Infinitive

111. The subject of an infinitive is in the objective case.

This construction will be treated in connection with the uses of the infinitive (§ 325).

Parsing

112. To **parse** a word is to describe its grammatical form and to give its construction.

In parsing a **noun**, we mention the class to which it belongs, give its gender, number, person, and case, and tell why it is in that case. Thus,—

1. Frank shot a wolf.

Frank is a proper noun of the masculine gender, in the singular number and third person. It is in the nominative case, because it is the subject of the verb *shot*.

Wolf is a common noun of the masculine or feminine [or common] gender, in the singular number and third person. It is in the objective case, because it is the object [or direct object] of the transitive verb *shot*.

2. Jane, come here.

Jane is a proper noun of the feminine gender, in the singular number and second person. It is in the nominative case, being used as a vocative (or in direct address).

3. The rope is fifteen feet long.

Feet is a common noun of the neuter gender, in the plural number and third person. It is in the objective case, being used as an adverbial modifier of the adjective *long*.

4. Edgar's boat is a sloop.

Edgar's is a proper noun of the masculine gender, in the singular number and third person. It is in the possessive case, modifying the noun *boat*.

CHAPTER III
PRONOUNS

113. A pronoun is a word used instead of a noun. It designates a person, place, or thing without naming it.

The substantive to which a pronoun refers is called its antecedent.

A pronoun must agree with its antecedent in gender, number, and person (§ 11).

Pronouns have in general the same constructions as nouns.

114. Pronouns may be classified as (1) **personal**, (2) **adjective**, (3) **relative**, and (4) **interrogative**.

Under adjective pronouns are included (*a*) **demonstrative pronouns** and (*b*) **indefinite pronouns**.

PERSONAL PRONOUNS

115. The personal pronouns serve to distinguish (1) the speaker, (2) the person spoken to, and (3) the person, place, or thing spoken of (§ 85).

They are declined as follows:—

THE PRONOUN OF THE FIRST PERSON: *I*

SINGULAR		PLURAL	
Nominative	I	*Nominative*	we
Possessive	my *or* mine	*Possessive*	our *or* ours
Objective	me	*Objective*	us

THE PRONOUN OF THE SECOND PERSON: *thou*

SINGULAR		PLURAL	
Nominative	thou	*Nominative*	you *or* ye
Possessive	thy *or* thine	*Possessive*	your *or* yours
Objective	thee	*Objective*	you *or* ye

THE PRONOUN OF THE THIRD PERSON: *he, she, it*

	SINGULAR			PLURAL
	MASCULINE	FEMININE	NEUTER	MASCULINE, FEMININE, and NEUTER
Nominative	he	she	it	they
Possessive	his	her *or* hers	its	their *or* theirs
Objective	him	her	it	them

Unlike nouns, most of the personal pronouns have distinct forms for the nominative and the objective.

NOTE. The possessive case of personal pronouns never has the apostrophe. Thus,—*its, yours, theirs.*

The form *it's* is proper only as a contraction of *it is.*

GENDER AND NUMBER

116. The pronouns of the first and second persons (*I* and *thou*) may be either masculine or feminine.

The pronouns of the third person have different forms for masculine, feminine, and neuter in the **singular** (*he, she, it*); but in the **plural** the form *they* serves for all three genders.

NOTE. In the oldest English *his* was both masculine and neuter. The neuter use lasted until the seventeenth century. Thus,—

> That same eye whose bend doth awe the world
> Did lose *his* lustre.—SHAKSPERE, *Julius Cæsar*, i. 2. 123.

117. *Thou, thy, thine, thee,* and *ye* are old forms still found in poetry and the solemn style.

In ordinary prose, *you, your,* and *yours* are the only forms used for the second person, whether singular or plural. Yet *you,* even when denoting a single person, always takes the verb-forms that go with plural subjects. Thus,—

> My friend, *you were* [NOT *was*] in error.

Hence *you* may best be regarded as always plural in form, but may be described as singular in sense when it stands for one person only.

NOTE. Members of the Society of Friends (commonly called Quakers) and of some other religious bodies use *thee* and *thy* in their ordinary conversation.

Ye was formerly the regular nominative plural, and *you* the objective; but the forms were afterwards confused. *Ye* has gone out of use except in poetry and the solemn style, and *you* is now the regular form for both nominative and objective.

Where an objective form *ye* is found printed instead of *you* (as often in Shakspere,—"A southwest blow on *ye*"), it represents an indistinct pronunciation of *you* rather than the old nominative *ye*. This indistinct sound may still be heard in rapid or careless speech ("I'll tell yer the truth").

Ye as an abbreviation for *the* (as in "*ye* old town") has nothing to do with the pronoun *ye*. The *y* simply stands for the character þ (an old sign for *th*), and the abbreviation was pronounced *the*, never *ye*.

118. *They, you,* and *we* are often used indefinitely for "one" or "people in general."

> *They* say that Joe has gone to sea.
> To shut off the steam, *you* close both valves of the radiator.

NOTE. *We, our,* and *us* are used in editorial articles instead of *I, my,* and *me,* because the writer represents the whole editorial staff. This practice should not be followed in ordinary composition.

A sovereign ruler may use *we, our,* and *us* when speaking of himself in proclamations and other formal documents. This construction is often called "the plural of majesty." Thus,—

> Know that *we* have divided
> In three *our* kingdom.—SHAKSPERE.

The form *'em* (as in "Tell me your counsels; I will not disclose *'em,*" in *Julius Cæsar*) is not a contraction of *them,* but of *hem,* an old objective plural of *he.*

CASE OF PERSONAL PRONOUNS

NOMINATIVE CASE

119. Nominative constructions of the personal pronouns are the same as those of nouns (§ 88).

> *I* am ready. [Subject.]
> It is *I.* [Predicate nominative.]
> Here, *you* rascal, what are you about? [Vocative, direct address.]
> Poor *you*! [Nominative of exclamation.]
> General Austin, *he* and no other, won the battle. [Apposition.]

For the **nominative absolute**, see § 345.

Care must be taken not to use an objective form when a predicate nominative is required.

> It is *I* [NOT *me*].
> It is *we* [NOT *us*] who did it.
> It was *he* [NOT *him*] who told us.
> It was *they* [NOT *them*] who were to blame.

120. *It* has several peculiar uses in the nominative.

1. *It* is used as the subject in many expressions like "It rains," "It snows," "It lightens," "It is cold," where no definite subject is thought of. In this use, *it* is said to be **impersonal**.

> NOTE. An impersonal *it* also occurs as a cognate object (§ 108) in colloquial language: as,—"Hang it!" "Go it!" "He went it." "He farmed it for a year." Other examples of the indefinite and impersonal *it* in various constructions are: "We are roughing *it*." "Keep *it* up." "You'll catch *it*." "Let *it* all go." "He made a poor job of *it*." "He made a success of *it*."

2. *It* often serves as grammatical subject merely to introduce the verb *is*, the real subject of the thought standing in the predicate. In this use *it* is called an **expletive** (or "filler").

> *It* is he.
> *It* is Christmas.
> *It* was a tiresome ride.

In these examples, the subject of the thought (*he, Christmas, ride*) appears as a predicate nominative.

3. The antecedent of *it* is often a group of words.

> Wearing tight shoes is foolish. *It* deforms the feet.

121. In **imperative sentences** the subject (*you*) is commonly omitted: as,—"Shut the door."

> NOTE. The subject *I* is sometimes omitted in wishes (as, "*Would* he were here!" for "I would that he were here"). So also in "Thank you," "Pray tell me" (compare *prithee* for "I pray thee").
> Expressions like "Canst tell?" (for "Canst thou tell?"), "Art there?" (for "Art thou there?") are common in poetry and older English. These come from the gradual wearing away and final disappearance of the pronoun *thou* (*canst thou, canstow, canstë, canst*).

POSSESSIVE CASE

122. The **possessive** forms *my, thy, our, your, her,* and *their* are used when a noun follows; *mine, thine, ours, yours, hers,* and *theirs* cannot be followed by a noun, and stand commonly in the predicate. *His* may be used in either way.

My brother has arrived.	The fault is *mine.*
Our work is done.	Those seats are *ours.*
I have torn *your* glove.	This pencil is *yours.*
Their turn has come.	That field is *theirs.*
His hair is black.	The book is not *his.*

Examples of *mine, yours,* etc. not in the predicate are:

Mine was a terrier; *yours* was a pointer.
Theirs is a red motor car.
Ours broke down last night.
His leaked badly.
His name is Martin; *hers* is Smith.

In such cases the pronoun is always emphatic. The construction is chiefly colloquial.

NOTE. In older English and in poetry *mine* and *thine* are common instead of *my* and *thy* before words beginning with a vowel or *h*: as,—

Mine eyes dazzle: she died young.—JOHN WEBSTER.
The very minute bids thee ope *thine* ear.—SHAKSPERE.

Mine is sometimes used after a vocative noun: as,—*brother mine.*
For expressions like "a friend of *mine,*" "that unruly tongue of *yours,*" see §96.

123. When two or more separate objects are spoken of as possessed, a possessive should precede the name of each if there is danger of ambiguity.

I will send for our secretary and our treasurer. [Two persons.]

I will send for our secretary and treasurer. [One person.]

I have called for my bread and my milk. [Two things.]

I have called for my bread and milk. [A mixture.]

Have you Bacon's "Essays and Apophthegms"? [One book.]

Have you Bacon's "Essays" and his "Advancement of Learning"? [Two books.]

Objective Case

124. The commonest constructions in which personal pronouns take the **objective case** are the following:—

1. Object of a preposition (§ 97): as,—

Take it from *him.*

2. Direct object of a transitive verb (§ 99): as,—

I will find *you.*

3. Indirect object of a transitive verb (§ 105): as,—

He gave *me* a dollar.

4. Subject of an infinitive (see § 325).

NOTE. In poetry the objective *me* is sometimes used in exclamations: as,—"*Me* miserable!" (MILTON).

In *methinks* and *meseems* ("it seems to me"), *me* is a remnant of the old dative, as in the indirect object (see § 107).

The compounds *thereof, therewith, therefrom,* etc., are equivalent to *of it, with it, from it,* etc.: as, —"Proclaim liberty throughout all the land unto all the inhabitants *thereof*" (*Leviticus* xxv. 10).

For the impersonal *it* as cognate object, see § 120.

THE *SELF*-PRONOUNS (COMPOUND PERSONAL PRONOUNS)

125. The three **compound personal pronouns** are made by adding the word *self* to certain forms of the personal pronouns. Thus,—

myself, *plural* ourselves;
thyself *or* yourself, *plural* yourselves;
himself, herself, itself, *plural* themselves.

> To these may be added the indefinite *oneself*, more commonly written as two words, *one's self* (§ 139).

Observe that *yourself* is singular, and *yourselves* plural. *Hisself* and *theirselves* are incorrect forms. *Ourself* (not *ourselves*) is the compound pronoun corresponding to the royal *we* (§ 118).

What touches us *ourself* shall be last served.—SHAKSPERE.

126. 1. **The compound personal pronouns may be used to emphasize substantives.**
In this use they are called intensive pronouns.

I *myself* will go.
King Alfred *himself* took the field.
They did the work *themselves*.

An intensive pronoun is in apposition with the substantive to which it refers.

2. **The compound personal pronouns may be used as the objects of transitive verbs or of prepositions when the object denotes the same person or thing as the subject.**
In this use they are called reflexive pronouns.

I have hurt *myself.*

King Alfred interested *himself* in his subjects.

These schemers deceived *themselves.*

Mary was talking to *herself.*

He gave *himself* a holiday. [Indirect object.]

These pronouns are called **reflexive** (that is, "bending back") because they **refer back** to the subject and repeat its meaning in an object construction.

NOTE. A reflexive pronoun sometimes refers to a substantive in the objective case: as,—"Our captors left *us* to *ourselves.*"

In older English the simple personal pronouns *me, thee,* etc., were often used reflexively: as,—"I held *me* [= *myself*] still"; "Yield *thee* [= *thyself*] captive"; "They built *them* [= for *themselves*] houses" (see § 106). This idiom survives in colloquial language (as, "I have hurt *me,*" "I have bought *me* a rifle"), but it is avoided in writing except in a few expressions such as: "I must look about *me*"; "We gazed about *us*"; "Look behind *you.*"

127. The adjective *own* is sometimes inserted between the first and the second part of the *self*-pronouns for emphasis.

EXAMPLES: my own self, your own self, his own self, our own selves, their own selves.

In this use, *self* is in strictness a noun limited by the possessive and by the adjective *own,* but the phrases may be regarded as compound pronouns. Other adjectives are sometimes inserted between the possessive and *self*: as,—my *very* self, his *worthless* self.

128. The intensive pronouns are sometimes used without a substantive. Thus,—

It is *myself.* [*Myself* = *I myself.*]

You are hardly *yourself* to-day.

In poetry and older English, the intensives are even found as subjects: as,—"*Ourself* will mingle with society" (*Macbeth*).

129. The intensive pronouns should not be used as simple personal pronouns.

> Thus we should say:—"He was kind to Mary and *me*" (NOT *myself*); "They invited my wife and *me* (NOT *myself*)."

ADJECTIVE PRONOUNS

130. Some words are used either as adjectives or as pronouns. Such words are called adjective pronouns.

Adjective pronouns are classified, according to their meaning, as (1) **demonstrative pronouns** and (2) **indefinite pronouns**.

I. DEMONSTRATIVE PRONOUNS

131. The demonstratives are *this* (plural, *these*), *that* (plural, *those*). They point out persons or things for special attention.

The demonstratives may be used either as adjectives or as pronouns.

I. As adjectives:—

This sailor saved my life.	*These* girls are energetic.
Be kind to *this* child.	I am not alarmed by *these* threats.
Give *this* boy a dime.	*These* cherries are sour.
This fire is too hot.	Look at *these* acorns.
That saw is dull.	*Those* trees are dying.
We must cross *that* stream.	Take *those* dishes away.
That train is late.	Who are *those* strangers?
Send *that* dog home.	Do you see *those* rocks?
I am tired of *that* tune.	I am sorry for *those* children.

II. As pronouns:—

This is a fine morning.[19]	*These* are cowboys.
This is my uncle.	Robert gave me *these*.
Can you do *this*?	I never saw *these* before.
This is the road.	Who are *these*?
Look at *this*.	*These* are our rackets.
That is Ellen in the canoe.	*Those* are deer.
That would please him.	*Those* are nasturtiums.
That must be he.	What are *those*?
What is *that*?	*Those* are kangaroos.

If the demonstrative is followed by a noun which it limits (as in "*this* sailor"), it is an adjective. If the demonstrative points out something which it does not name (as in "*This* is a fine morning"), it takes the place of a noun and is therefore a pronoun. The simple subject of the sentence "This camera is expensive" is the noun *camera*, which is modified by the adjective *this*. The subject of the sentence "*This* is expensive" is the pronoun *this*.

NOTE. *Yon, yond,* and *yonder* are common as demonstratives in older English and in poetry. Thus,—"Nerissa, cheer *yon* stranger" (*Merchant of Venice*). "Question *yond* man" (*As You Like It*). "Is not *yond* Diomed?" (*Troilus and Cressida*). "Call *yonder* fellow hither" (*Henry V*). "Is *yonder* the man?" (*As You Like It*).

132. Demonstratives have only the inflection of number. They have the same form for all three genders. The nominative and objective cases are alike; the possessive is replaced by *of* with the objective.

SINGULAR		PLURAL	
Nom. and Obj.	this	*Nom. and Obj.*	these
Possessive	[of this]	*Possessive*	[of these]
Nom. and Obj.	that	*Nom. and Obj.*	those
Possessive	[of that]	*Possessive*	[of those]

Yon, yond, and *yonder* are not inflected.

133. A demonstrative pronoun may be used to avoid the repetition of a noun.

> My dog and *that* [= the dog] of my friend John have been fighting.
>
> Compare these maps with *those* [= the maps] on the blackboard.

134. The singular forms *this* and *that* (not the plurals *these* and *those*) are used with the nouns *kind* and *sort.*

> I like *this* kind of grapes.
> I have met *this* sort of people before.
> *That* kind of apples grows in Idaho.

II. INDEFINITE PRONOUNS

135. The indefinite pronouns point out objects less clearly or definitely than demonstratives do.

> Examples: each, every, either, both, neither, some, any, such, none, other, another, each other, one another.

> *Each* has its merits.
> *Some* are missing.
> I cannot give you *any.*
> *Either* is correct.
> He knows *neither* of you.
> I like *both.*

136. Most indefinites may be either **pronouns** or **adjectives**. But *none* is always a substantive in modern use, and *every* is always an adjective.

137. *None* may be either singular or plural. When it means distinctly *not one*, it is singular. In many instances either construction is permissible.

> *None* of us has the key.
> *None* was (*or* were) left to tell the tale.

138. *Each other* and *one another* are regarded as **compound** pronouns. They designate related persons or things.

> My neighbor and I like *each other*.
> We must bear with *one another*.

The relation indicated by these pronouns is that of reciprocity. Hence they are often called reciprocal pronouns.

There is no real distinction between *each other* and *one another*. The rules sometimes given for such a distinction are not supported by the best usage.

139. *One* (possessive *one's*) is often used as an indefinite personal pronoun. Thus,—

> *One* does not like *one's* [NOT *his* or *their*] motives to be doubted.

The use of *his* (for *one's*) to refer back to a preceding *one* is found in respectable writers, but is contrary to the best usage.

For the indefinite use of *we, you, they*, see § 118.

140. *All, several, few, many,* and similar words are often classed as indefinites. They may be used as adjectives or as substantives. *Everybody, everything, anybody, anything, somewhat, aught, naught,*[20] etc., are called indefinite nouns.

141. Care should be taken in framing such sentences as the following:—

> Everybody has *his* [NOT *their*] faults.
> If anybody wishes to go, *he* [NOT *they*] may.
> If anybody objects, let *him* [NOT *them*] speak.

Every member of this class must hand in *his* [NOT *their*] composition to-day.

Each hurries toward *his* [NOT *their*] home.

Each of us must lead *his* [NOT *their*] own life.

In sentences of this kind, the personal pronoun (*he, his, him*) must be in the singular to agree with its antecedent (*everybody, anybody*, etc.) (see § 113).

> NOTE. When the antecedent is of common gender (as in the last example), the personal pronouns (*he, his, him*) may be regarded as of common gender also. In very precise or formal language, one may say *he or she, his or her*: as,—"Each of us must lead *his or her* own life"; but this form of expression is to be avoided unless the distinction is clearly necessary.

142. When used as adjectives, none of the indefinites have any forms of inflection. The same is true when they are pronouns, except as follows:—

> *Others* is used as the plural of *another*. The possessive forms are:—singular, *another's*; plural, *others'*. *The other* (possessive, *the other's*) has in the plural *the others* (possessive, *the others'*). *Each other* and *one another* add *'s* in the possessive. *One* has a possessive *one's*; *the one* becomes *the ones* in the plural.

RELATIVE PRONOUNS

143. Relative pronouns have a peculiar function in the sentence, since they serve both as **pronouns** and as **connectives**. Their use may be seen by comparing the two sentences that follow:—

1. This is the sailor, and he saved my life.
2. This is the sailor who saved my life.

Each consists of two parts or clauses (§ 44). In No. 1, the two clauses are connected by the conjunction *and*, which belongs to neither; the pronoun *he*, which stands for *sailor*, is the subject of the second clause. In No. 2, there is no conjunction; instead, we find the word *who*, which replaces *and he*. This *who* is a **pronoun**, since it stands for *sailor* (precisely as *he* does in No. 1) and (like *he*) is the subject of the verb *saved*. But *who* is also a **connective**, since it joins the two parts of the sentence as *and* does in No. 1. Such words (which serve both as pronouns and as connectives) are called **relative pronouns**.

In No. 1, the two clauses are **coördinate**. Neither serves as a modifier, and each might stand alone as a complete sentence ("This is the sailor." "He saved my life"). The sentence is compound (§ 44). In No. 2, on the contrary, the clause *who saved my life* is a **subordinate** or **dependent clause**, for it is used as an adjective modifier of the noun *sailor*, which it limits by showing what particular sailor is meant. The sentence is **complex** (§ 44). The dependent clause (*who saved my life*) is connected with the main clause (*this is the sailor*) by the pronoun *who*, which refers to *sailor*.

144. Relative pronouns connect dependent clauses with main clauses by referring directly to a substantive in the main clause.[21]

This substantive is the antecedent of the relative (§ 11).

Thus in § 143 the noun *sailor* is the antecedent of *who*.

> *Relative* means "carrying back." These pronouns are so called because they carry the mind back directly to the antecedent.

145. The simple relative pronouns are *who, which, that, as,* and *what.*

Who and *which* are declined as follows in both the singular and the plural:—

Nominative	who	which
Possessive	whose	whose
Objective	whom	which

That, as, and *what* are not inflected. They have the same form for both nominative and objective and are not used in the possessive case.

146. *As* may be used as a relative pronoun when *such* stands in the main clause.

> Such of you *as* have finished may go.
> I have never seen such strawberries *as* these [are].
> Use such powers *as* you have.

147. *As* is often used as a relative after *the same.*

> This color is the same *as* that [is].

Other relatives are also used after *the same.*

> This is the same book *that* (or *which*) you were reading yesterday.
> This is the same man *that* (or *whom*) I saw on the pier last Friday.

148. *Who* is either masculine or feminine; *which* and *what* are neuter; *that* and *as* are of all three genders.

> All *who* heard, approved.
> Here is the lad *whose* story interested you.
> The first woman *whom* I saw was Mary.
> He answered in such English *as* he could muster.
> I saw nobody *that* I knew.
> This is the road *that* leads to London.

In older English *the which* is often used for *which*: as,—

> Our foster-nurse of nature is repose,
> *The which* he lacks.—SHAKSPERE.

For other uses of *as*, see §§ 368, 428–429. For *but* in such sentences as "There was nobody *but* believed him," see § 370.

149. A relative pronoun must agree with its antecedent in gender, number, and person.

The sentences in § 148 illustrate the agreement of the relative with its antecedent in **gender**.

Since relative pronouns have the same form for both numbers and for all three persons, their **number and person** must be discovered, in each instance, by observing the number and person of the **antecedent**.

It is *I who am* wrong. [First person, singular number: antecedent, *I*.]

All *you who are* ready may go. [Second person plural: antecedent, *you*.]

Give help to *him who needs it*. [Third person, singular: antecedent, *him*.]

The *road that leads* to the shore is sandy. [Third person singular: antecedent, *road*.]

The *roads that lead* to the shore are sandy. [Third person plural: antecedent, *roads*.]

To determine the number and person of a relative pronoun is particularly necessary when it is the **subject of the clause**, for the form of the verb varies (as the examples show) according to the number and person of the subject (§ 222). Hence the rule for the agreement of a relative with its antecedent is of much practical importance.

150. The case of a relative pronoun has nothing to do with its antecedent, but depends on the construction of its own clause.

The servant *who* opened the door wore livery. [*Who* is in the nominative case, being the subject of *opened*.]

He discharged his servant, *who* immediately left town. [*Who* is in the nominative case, since it is the subject of *left*, although its antecedent (*servant*) is in the objective.]

The servant *whom* you discharged has returned. [*Whom* is in the objective case, since it is the direct object of *discharged*. The antecedent (*servant*) is, on the other hand, in the nominative, because it is the subject of *has returned*.]

Here is such money *as* I have. [*As* is in the objective case, being the object of *have*. The antecedent (*money*) is in the nominative.]

151. A relative pronoun in the objective case is often omitted.

Here is the book *which* you wanted.	Here is the book you wanted.
The noise *that* I heard was the wind.	The noise I heard was the wind.
The man *whom* I met was a carpenter.	The man I met was a carpenter.

NOTE. In older English a relative in the nominative is often omitted: as,—"There's two or three of us *have* seen strange sights" (*Julius Cæsar*), that is, "There are two or three of us *who have* seen," etc. The same omission is often made in rapid or careless colloquial speech. It is approved in clauses with *there* in such sentences as "He is one of the best men there are in the world" (§ 232).

152. Certain questions of **gender** call for particular attention.

1. *Which* is commonly used in referring to the lower animals unless these are regarded as persons. This is true even when *he* or *she* is used of the same animals (§ 69).

This is the dog *which* I mentioned. Isn't *he* a fine fellow?

We have one cow *which* we prize highly. *She* is a Jersey.

2. The possessive *whose* may be used of any object that has life.

> This is the man *whose* watch was stolen.
> I have a cat *whose* name is Tabby.
> This is the tree *whose* leaves were destroyed. *It* is quite dead.

3. In the case of things without animal life, *of which* and *whose* are both common. The tendency is to prefer *of which* in prose, but *whose* is often used because of its more agreeable sound. In poetry, *whose* is especially frequent.

> A broad river, the name *of which* I have forgotten, forms the northern boundary of the province.
>
> Jack was fishing with a bamboo rod, to the end *of which* he had tied a short piece of ordinary twine.
>
> She was gazing into the pool, *whose* calm surface reflected her features like a mirror. ["The surface *of which*" would not sound so well.]

NOTE. In older English, *which* is often used for *who* or *whom*: as,—"He *which* hath your noble father slain, pursued my life" (*Hamlet*).

The compounds *whereof, wherefrom, wherewith*, etc., are equivalent to *of which, from which*, etc. (cf. § 124). Thus,—"Esau hated Jacob because of the blessing *wherewith* his father blessed him" (*Genesis* xxvii. 41).

DESCRIPTIVE AND RESTRICTIVE RELATIVES

153. The clause introduced by a relative pronoun is an **adjective clause**, since it serves as an adjective modifier of the antecedent (§ 143). There are two different ways in which the antecedent may be thus modified.

> 1. The Italian, *who wore a flower in his coat*, smiled at me.
> 2. The Italian *who wore a flower in his coat* smiled at me.

In the first sentence, the italicized relative clause serves simply to **describe** the Italian, not to identify him. The flower is a mere detail of the picture.

In the second sentence, the relative clause serves not merely to describe the Italian, but also to distinguish him from all others. The flower is mentioned as a means of **identification**. The relative clause confines or **restricts** the meaning of the antecedent (*Italian*).

154. A relative pronoun that serves merely to introduce a descriptive fact is called a descriptive relative.

A relative pronoun that introduces a clause confining or limiting the application of the antecedent is called a restrictive relative.

Thus in the first example in § 153, *who* is a descriptive relative; in the second, it is a restrictive relative.

155. Before a descriptive relative we regularly make a pause in speaking, but never before a restrictive relative. Hence the rule:—

A descriptive relative is preceded by a comma; a restrictive relative is not.

> Three sailors, *who* were loitering on the pier, sprang to the rescue.
>
> A clumsy weapon, *which* I took for a blunderbuss, hung over the fireplace.
>
> I told the news to the first man *that* (or *whom*) I met.
>
> The coins *that* (or *which*) you showed me are doubloons.
>
> Nothing *that* I have ever read has moved me more profoundly than the third act of "King Lear."

156. *Who*, *which*, and *that* are all used as restrictive relatives; but some writers prefer *that* to *which*, especially in the nominative case.

NOTE. *That* is not now employed as a descriptive relative, though it was common in this use not very long ago. Thus in 1844 Disraeli wrote: "The deer, *that* abounded, lived here in a world as savage as themselves" (*Coningsby*, book iii, chapter 5).

The omission of the relative (§ 151) is possible only when the relative is restrictive.

> The boy [*whom*] I saw at your house has left town. [Restrictive.]
>
> Charles, *whom* I saw yesterday, had not heard the news. [Descriptive.]

THE RELATIVE PRONOUN *WHAT*

157. The relative pronoun *what* is equivalent to *that which*, and has a **double construction**:—(1) the construction of the **omitted** or **implied antecedent** (*that*); (2) the construction of the **relative** (*which*).

> {*What* | *That which*} was said is true. [Here *what*, being equivalent to *that which*, serves as the subject both of *was said* and of *is*.]
>
> Tom always remembers {*what* | *that which*} is said to him. [Here *what*, being equivalent to *that which*, serves as both the object of *remembers* and as the subject of *is said*.]
>
> Tom always remembers {*what* | *that which*} he learns. [Here *what* serves both as the object of *remembers* and as the object of *learns*.]

In parsing *what*, mention both of its constructions.

NOTE. Another method of dealing with the relative *what* is to regard the whole clause (*what was said*; *what is said to him*; *what he learns*) as a **noun clause**. Thus the clause *what was said* in the first sentence would be the subject of *is*; in the second and third sentences, the clause would be the object of *remembers*. *What*, in the first sentence, would be parsed as the subject of *was said*; in the second, as the subject of *is said*; and in the third, as the object of *learns*. Neither view is incorrect, and each has its special advantages.

The student may well be familiar with both methods, remembering that grammar cannot be treated like mathematics.

COMPOUND RELATIVE PRONOUNS

158. The compound relative pronouns are formed by adding *ever* or *soever* to *who, which,* and *what.*

They are declined as follows:—

SINGULAR AND PLURAL

Nominative	whoever (whosoever)	whichever (whichsoever)
Possessive	whosever (whosesoever)	————
Objective	whomever (whomsoever)	whichever (whichsoever)

Whatever (*whatsoever*) has no inflection. The nominative and the objective are alike, and the possessive is supplied by the phrase *of whatever* (*of whatsoever*).

The phrase *of whichever* (*of whichsoever*) is used instead of *whosever* exactly as *of which* is used instead of *whose* (§ 152).

159. The compound relative pronouns may include or imply their own antecedents and hence may have a double construction.

Whoever calls, *he* must be admitted. [Here *he*, the antecedent of *whoever*, is the subject of *must be admitted*, and *whoever* is the subject of *calls*.]

Whoever calls must be admitted. [Here the antecedent *he* is omitted, being implied in *whoever*. *Whoever* has therefore a double construction, being the subject of both *calls* and *must be admitted*.]

He shall have *whatever* he wishes.

I will do *whichever* you say.

In such sentences, care should be taken to use *whoever* and *whomever* correctly. The nominative (*whoever*) is required when the relative is the subject of its own clause.

He asked *whoever* came.
He told the story to *whoever* would listen.
He asked *whomever* he knew.
He told the story to *whomever* he met.

160. The compound relatives are sometimes used without an antecedent expressed or implied.

Whoever deserts you, I will remain faithful.
Whomever it offends, I will speak the truth.
Whatever he attempts, he is sure to fail.
Whichever you choose, you will be disappointed.

NOTE. This construction is closely related to that explained in § 159. "Whoever deserts you, I will remain faithful," is practically equivalent to "Whoever deserts you, let him desert you! I will remain faithful." No antecedent, however, is felt by the speaker, and hence none need be supplied in parsing. Compare concessive clauses (§ 401).

161. *Which, what, whichever,* and *whatever* are often used as adjectives.

Use *what* (or *whatever*) powers you have.
Whichever plan you adopt, you have my best wishes.

162. A noun limited by the adjectives *what, whichever,* and *whatever,* may have the same double construction that these relatives have when they are used as pronouns (§ 159). Thus,—

Take *whichever* pen is not in use. [Here *pen* is both the direct object of *take,* and the subject of *is.*]

Whoso for *whosoever* and *whatso* for *whatsoever* are common in older English.

INTERROGATIVE PRONOUNS

163. The interrogative pronouns are *who, which,* and *what.* They are used in asking questions.[22]

Who is your neighbor?

Who goes there?

Whom have you chosen?

From *whom* did you learn this?

Whose voice is that?

Which shall I take?

Which is correct?

What did he say?

What is lacking?

With *what* are you so delighted?

164. *Who* has a possessive *whose,* and an objective *whom. Which* and *what* are not inflected.

Who may be either masculine or feminine; *which* and *what* may be of any gender.

165. The **objective** *whom* often begins a question (as in the third example in § 163). Care should be taken not to write *who* for *whom.*

166. *Which* and *what* are used as **interrogative adjectives**.

Which street shall I take?

What village is this?

167. The interrogative adjective *what* may be used in a peculiar form of exclamatory sentence. Thus,—

> *What* a cold night this is!
> *What* courage he must have had!

What! by itself often serves as an exclamation: as,—"*What!* do you really think so?" In this use *what* may be regarded as an interjection.

168. In **parsing pronouns** the following models may be used:—

1. *He* was my earliest friend.

He is a personal pronoun of the third person. It is in the masculine gender, the singular number, and the nominative case, being the subject of the verb *was*.

2. A policeman *whom* I met showed me the house.

Whom is a relative pronoun of the masculine gender, singular number, and third person, agreeing with its antecedent, *policeman*. It is in the objective case, being the direct object of the transitive verb *met*.

3. The corporal, *whose* name was Scott, came from Leith.

Whose is a relative pronoun of the masculine gender, singular number, and third person, agreeing with its antecedent, *corporal*. It is in the possessive case, modifying the noun *name*.

4. *Whose* birthday do we celebrate in February?

Whose is an interrogative pronoun in the masculine or feminine gender, singular number, and possessive case, modifying the noun *birthday*.

5. He injured *himself* severely.

Himself is a compound personal pronoun of the third person, used reflexively. It is of the masculine gender, singular number, and third person, agreeing with its antecedent, *he*. It is in the objective case, being the direct object of the transitive verb *injured*.

CHAPTER IV
ADJECTIVES

CLASSIFICATION OF ADJECTIVES

169. An adjective is a word which describes or limits a substantive.

An adjective is said to belong to the substantive which it describes or limits.

An adjective which describes is called a descriptive adjective; one which points out or designates is called a definitive adjective (§ 13).

Most adjectives are descriptive: as,—*round, cold, red, angry, graceful, excessive, young, sudden, Roman.*

> NOTE. Many descriptive adjectives are **compound** (see § 64): as,—steadfast, lionlike, fireproof, downright, heartsick, everlasting, brown-eyed, broad-shouldered, ill-tempered, dear-bought, far-fetched, never-ending, self-evident, self-important. "He was a *matter-of-fact* person." "Tom is *hail-fellow-well-met* with everybody." "This is an *out-of-the-way* place." "A dashing, *down-at-the-heel* youth answered my knock."

170. A proper noun used as an adjective, or an adjective derived from a proper noun, is called a **proper adjective** and usually begins with a capital letter.

> EXAMPLES: a *Panama* hat, *Florida* oranges, a *Bunsen* burner; Virginian, Spenserian, Newtonian, Icelandic, Miltonic, Byronic, Turkish, English, Veronese.

> NOTE. Many so-called proper adjectives begin with a small letter because their origin is forgotten or disregarded: as,—*china* dishes, *italic* type, *mesmeric* power, a *jovial* air, a *saturnine* expression, a *mercurial* temperament, a *stentorian* voice.

171. Definitive adjectives include:—pronouns used as adjectives (as, *this* opportunity; *those* pictures; *either* table; *what* time is it?); numeral adjectives (as, *two* stars; the *third* year); the **articles**, *a* (or *an*) and *the*.

Pronouns used as adjectives (often called pronominal adjectives) have been studied under Pronouns—demonstratives (§§ 131–134), indefinites (§§ 135–142), relatives (§§ 143–162), interrogatives (§§ 163–167).

Numeral adjectives will be treated, along with other numerals (nouns and adverbs), in §§ 204–208.

The articles will be treated in §§ 173–180.

172. Adjectives may be classified, according to their position in the sentence, as **attributive**, **appositive**, and **predicate adjectives**.

1. An **attributive adjective** is closely attached to its noun and regularly precedes it.

> The *angry* spot doth glow on Cæsar's brow.
> O you *hard* hearts, you *cruel* men of Rome!
> *Yond* Cassius has a *lean* and *hungry* look.

2. An **appositive adjective** is added to its noun to explain it, like a noun in apposition (§ 88, 5).

Noun in Apposition	Appositive Adjective
The castle, a *ruin*, stood on the edge of the cliff.	The castle, *ancient* and *ruinous*, stood on the edge of the cliff.
Bertram, the *ringleader*, refused to surrender.	Bertram, *undaunted*, refused to surrender.

3. A **predicate adjective** completes the meaning of the predicate verb, but describes or limits the subject.

Predicate adjectives are common after *is* (in its various forms) and other copulative verbs, particularly *become* and *seem* (§ 17).

> The sea is *rough* to-day.
> Burton soon became *cautious* in his judgments.
> You seem *anxious* about your future.
> The air grew *hot* and *sultry*.
> Our first experiment proved *unsuccessful*.
> The milk turned *sour*.
> Our agent proved *trustworthy*.

NOTE. The construction of the predicate adjective is similar to that of the predicate nominative (§ 88, 2). Both are known as **complements**, because they complete the meaning of a verb.

After *look, sound, taste, smell, feel,* a predicate adjective is used to describe the subject. Thus,—

> Your flowers look *thrifty*. [NOT: look thriftily.]
> Their voices sound *shrill*. [NOT: sound shrilly.]
> This apple tastes *sweet*. [NOT: tastes sweetly.]
> The air smells *good*. [NOT: smells well.]
> The patient feels *comfortable*. [NOT: feels comfortably.]

For predicate adjectives after passive verbs, see § 492.
For the use of an adjective as predicate objective, see § 104.

THE ARTICLES

173. The adjectives *a* (or *an*) and *the* are called articles.

1. The definite article *the* points out one or more particular objects as distinct from others of the same kind.

The train is late.

Here is *the* key.

The children are in *the* next room.

2. **The indefinite article *a* (or *an*) designates an object as merely one of a general class or kind.**

Lend me *a* pencil.

I have *a* cold.

A young man answered my knock.

The article *a* is a fragment of *ān* (pronounced *ahn*), the ancient form of the numeral *one*; *an* keeps the *n*, which *a* has lost. *The* is an old demonstrative, related to *that*.

174. *The* with a singular noun sometimes indicates a **class** or **kind** of objects.

The scholar is not necessarily a dryasdust.

The elephant is the largest of quadrupeds.

The aëroplane is a very recent invention.

Resin is obtained from *the pine*.

NOTE. In this use *the* is often called the **generic article** (from the Latin *genus*, "kind" or "sort"). The singular number with the generic *the* is practically equivalent to the plural without an article. Thus in the first example the sense would be the same if we had, "*Scholars* are not necessarily dryasdusts."

175. An adjective preceded by *the* may be used as a plural noun.

The brave are honored.

The rich have many cares.

The strong should protect *the weak*.

176. *An* **is used before words beginning with a vowel or silent** *h*; *a* **before other words.** Thus,—

> *an* owl; *an* apple; *an* honest man; *a* stone; *a* pear.

177. Special rules for *a* or *an* are the following:—

1. Before words beginning with the sound of *y* or *w*, the form *a*, not *an*, is used.

> EXAMPLES: a union, a university, a yew, a ewe, a eulogy, a Utopian scheme, such a one.

> This rule covers all words beginning with *eu* and many beginning with *u*. Note that the initial sound is a consonant, not a vowel. *An* was formerly common before such words (as, —*an* union, such *an* one), but *a* is now the settled form.

2. Before words beginning with *h* and not accented on the first syllable, *an* is often used. Thus, we say—

> *a* his´tory; BUT, *an* histor´ical novel.

> In such cases, the *h* is very weak in sound, and is sometimes quite silent, so that the word practically begins with a vowel. Usage varies, but careful writers favor the rule here given. *An* was formerly more common before *h* than at present.

178. With two or more connected nouns or adjectives the article should be repeated whenever clearness requires (cf. § 123).

> I have consulted *the* secretary and *the* treasurer. ["The secretary and treasurer" would imply that the same person held both offices.]
> I found *an* anchor and *a* chain. ["An anchor and chain" would suggest that the chain was attached to the anchor.]
> In some towns there are separate schools for *the* boys and *the* girls; in others *the* boys and girls attend the same schools.
> He waved *a* red and white flag.

He waved *a* red and *a* white flag.

179. *A* is often used distributively, in the sense of *each*.

I paid five dollars *a* pair for my shoes.
The letter-carrier calls twice *a* day.
My class meets three times *a* week.

In such phrases *a* is better than *per*, except in strictly commercial language.

180. When used with adjectives, the articles precede, except in a few phrases: as,—

Such an uproar was never heard.
Many a man has tried in vain.

For the adverb *the*, which is quite distinct from the article in use and meaning, see § 195.
For the preposition *a* (as in "He went *a*-fishing"), see § 352.

COMPARISON OF ADJECTIVES

181. In **comparing** objects with each other, we may use three different forms of the same adjective.

Thomas is *strong*.
William is *stronger* than Thomas.
Herbert is *strongest* of the three.

This inflection of adjectives is called **comparison**, and the three forms are called **degrees of comparison**.

182. The degrees of comparison indicate by their form in what degree of intensity the quality described by the adjective exists.

There are three degrees of comparison,—the positive, the comparative, and the superlative.

1. **The positive degree is the simplest form of the adjective, and has no special ending.**

It merely describes the quality, without expressing or suggesting any comparison.

Thomas is *strong*.

Thus, the positive degree of the adjective *strong* is *strong*.

2. **The comparative degree of an adjective is formed by adding the termination *er* to the positive degree.**

It denotes that the quality exists in the object described in a higher degree than in some other object.

William is *stronger* than Thomas.

Thus, the comparative degree of the adjective *strong* is *stronger*.

3. **The superlative degree is formed by adding *est* to the positive degree.**

It denotes that the quality exists in the highest degree in the object described.

Herbert is *strongest* of the three.

Other examples of the **comparison of adjectives** are:—

Positive Degree	Comparative Degree	Superlative Degree
rich	richer	richest
poor	poorer	poorest
fast	faster	fastest
firm	firmer	firmest

183. RULES OF SPELLING.

1. Adjectives ending in silent *e* drop this letter before the comparative ending *er* and the superlative ending *est*. Thus,—

> wise, wiser, wisest; pure, purer, purest; handsome, handsomer, handsomest.

2. Most adjectives ending in *y* change *y* to *i* before the endings *er* and *est*. Thus,—

> silky, silkier, silkiest; glossy, glossier, glossiest; sorry, sorrier, sorriest.

3. Adjectives having a short vowel and ending in a single consonant double this before the endings *er* and *est*. Thus,—

> dim, dimmer, dimmest; sad, sadder, saddest; fit, fitter, fittest; big, bigger, biggest; red, redder, reddest; hot, hotter, hottest.

184. Many adjectives are compared by prefixing the adverbs *more* and *most* to the positive degree.

Many adjectives of two syllables and most adjectives of three or more syllables are so compared. Thus,—

> recent, more recent, most recent; terrible, more terrible, most terrible; triumphant, more triumphant, most triumphant; economical, more economical, most economical.

Some adjectives may be compared in either way.

> EXAMPLES: intense, intenser, intensest; OR intense, more intense, most intense. So also— profound, sublime, unkind.

IRREGULAR COMPARISON

185. Several adjectives have irregular comparison.[23]

POSITIVE	COMPARATIVE	SUPERLATIVE
bad (evil, ill)	worse	worst
far	farther	farthest
———	further	furthest
good	better	best
late	later, latter	latest, last
well (in health)	better	———
little	less, lesser	least
much, many	more	most

Old has comparative *older* or *elder*, superlative *oldest* or *eldest*. *Elder* or *eldest* may be used with certain nouns of relationship, or in the phrases *the elder* and *the eldest*.

This is my *elder* brother.	My brother is *older* than yours.
Jane was the *eldest* of six children.	I shall wear my *oldest* clothes.

Elder is also used as a noun: as,—"You should respect your *elders*."

Next is a superlative of *nigh*. It is used only in the sense of "the very nearest."

I live in the *next* street.

The *next* time he comes, I shall refuse to see him.

186. A few superlatives end in -*most*. With these, one or both of the other degrees are commonly wanting.

POSITIVE	COMPARATIVE	SUPERLATIVE
——	(former)	foremost
hind	hinder	hindmost
——	inner	inmost, innermost
(out, *adverb*)	outer	outmost, outermost
	(utter)	utmost, uttermost
(up, *adverb*)	upper	uppermost
——	——	endmost
——	nether	nethermost
top	——	topmost
——	——	furthermost
north	——	northmost
northern	(more northern)	northernmost
south	——	southmost
southern	(more southern)	southernmost
east, eastern	(more eastern)	easternmost
west, western	(more western)	westernmost

NOTE. The ending -*most* is not the adverb *most*. It is a very old superlative ending -*mest* changed under the influence of the adverb *most*.

187. For adjectives incapable of comparison, see § 202. For special rules for the use of comparative and superlative, see §§ 199–203.

CHAPTER V
ADVERBS

189. An adverb is a word which modifies a verb, an adjective, or another adverb.

> The storm ceased *suddenly*.
> A *very* disastrous storm swept the coast.
> The storm ceased *very* suddenly.

190. Adverbs are classified according to their meaning as: (1) adverbs of **manner**; (2) adverbs of **time**; (3) adverbs of **place**; (4) adverbs of **degree**.[24]

1. Adverbs of manner answer the question "How?" "In what way?"

They modify verbs or adjectives, rarely adverbs. Most of them are formed from adjectives by adding *ly*.

> Tom answered *courageously*.
> The poor child looked *helplessly* about.
> *Softly* and *silently* fell the snow.
> The pain was *terribly* severe.
> The river rose *surprisingly* fast.

2. Adverbs of time answer the question "When?" They usually modify verbs. Thus,—

> The old castle is *now* a museum.
> He was *recently* promoted.

I have been disturbed *lately*.

My friend arrives *to-day*.

James was *then* a boy of seven.

I have *already* rung the bell.

Afterwards he regretted his haste.

3. Adverbs of place answer the question "Where?" They usually modify verbs. Thus,—

Come *here*.

Yonder stands the culprit.

An old sailor came *forward*.

My sister is *out*.

I was *abroad* that winter.

4. Adverbs of degree answer the question "To what degree or extent?" They modify verbs, adjectives, and adverbs. Thus,—

Arthur is *rather* tall.

Father was *much* pleased.

Father was *very much* pleased.

The task seemed *utterly* hopeless.

That is *hardly* possible.

That is *not* possible.

191. Some adverbs have the same form as the corresponding adjectives.

You have guessed *right*.

How *fast* the tide ebbs!

The horse was sold *cheap*.

Tired men sleep *sound*.

Other examples are:— wrong, straight, early, late, quick, hard, far, near, slow, high, low, loud, ill, well, deep, close, just, very, much, little.

Under this head come certain adverbs of degree used to modify adjectives.

His eyes were *dark* blue. [Compare: *very* blue.]
That silk is *light* yellow. [Compare: *rather* yellow.]
These flowers are *deep* purple. [Compare: *intensely* purple.]
The water was *icy* cold. [Compare: *extremely* cold.]

That *dark*, *light*, etc., are adverbs in this use appears from the fact that they answer the question "How?" Thus,—"His eyes were blue." "*How* blue?" "*Dark* blue."

NOTE. In the oldest English many adverbs ended in -*ë*, as if formed directly from adjectives by means of this ending. Thus, the adjective for *hot* was *hāt*, side by side with which was an adverb *hātë* (dissyllabic), meaning *hotly*. In the fourteenth century this distinction was still kept up. Thus, Chaucer used both the adjective *hōt* and the dissyllabic adverb *hōtë*, meaning *hotly*. Between 1400 and 1500 all weak final *e*'s disappeared from the language. In this way the adverb *hotë*, for example, became simply *hot*. Thus these adverbs in -*ë* became identical in form with the corresponding adjectives. Hence in the time of Shakspere there existed, in common use, not only the adjective *hot*, but also the adverb *hot* (identical in form with the adjective but really descended from the adverb *hotë*). One could say not only "The fire is *hot*" (adjective), but "The fire burns *hot*" (adverb of manner).

The tendency in modern English has been to confine the form without ending to the adjective use and to restrict the adverbial function to forms in -*ly*. Thus, a writer of the present time would not say, in prose, "The fire burns *hot*," but "The fire burns *hotly*." Nevertheless, a number of the old adverbs without ending still remain in good use, and must not be regarded as erroneous.

In poetry, moreover, such adverbs are freely employed; as,—"The boy like a gray goshawk stared *wild*." [In prose: stared *wildly*.]

For adverbial phrases, see §§ 41–42, 475.
For the adverbial objective, see § 109.
192. *Yes* and *no* are peculiar adverbs used in assenting and denying. Thus,—

Are you hungry?

No.

NOTE. As now used, *yes* and *no* stand for complete sentences. Originally, however, they were modifiers, and hence they are still classed as adverbs. The original meaning of *no* was "never." Compare *never* as an emphatic negative in modern English: as,—"Will you surrender?" "*Never!*" The oldest affirmative adverb was *yea*. *Yes* was originally a compound of *yea* with a form of *so*, and was used in emphatic affirmatives (like our *just so!*).

Other adverbs or adverbial phrases are sometimes used like *yes* or *no*. Such are *certainly, assuredly, by no means, not at all*. In these cases, however, the modifying effect of the word or phrase may easily be seen when the sentence is supplied. Thus,—"Will you help me?" "*Certainly* [I *will help* you]."

193. *There* is often used merely to introduce a sentence in the inverted order (§ 5).

> There is a hole in my shoe.
>
> There are many strangers in town.
>
> There rose a thick smoke from the volcano.

In this use, *there* is sometimes called an **expletive** (or "filler"). It is unemphatic, and has lost all its force as an adverb of place. Contrast "THERE [emphatic] stood an Indian under a tree" with, "There [unemphatic expletive] stood an Indian under a tree."

RELATIVE AND INTERROGATIVE ADVERBS

194. Relative adverbs introduce subordinate clauses and are similar in their use to relative pronouns.

> I know a farmhouse {in which | *where*} we can spend the night.

Where is an adverb of place, modifying *can spend*. But it also introduces the subordinate clause, as the relative pronoun *which* does.

Hence *where* is called a **relative adverb**.

195. The principal relative adverbs are:—*where, whence, whither, wherever, when, whenever, while, as, how, why, before, after, till, until, since.*

> Because of their similarity to conjunctions, these words are often called **conjunctive adverbs**.

He had a fever *when* he was in Spain.

Work *while* it is day.

As the ship passed, we observed that her decks were crowded with Malays. [Time.]

Keep to the right, *as* the law directs. [Manner.]

You started *before* I was ready.

Wait *until* the car stops.

Since you came, it has rained constantly.

> *As* and *since* in the sense of "because," and *while* in the sense of "although," are classed as conjunctions (§ 368).

The clauses introduced by relative adverbs may be either adjective or adverbial (§§ 49–50, 379–382).

> NOTE. In "*The* more you waste, *the* sooner you will want" (and similar sentences) *the* is not an article, but an old case-form of the pronoun *that*, used as an adverb of degree. We may expand the sentence as follows: "*To what extent* you waste more, *to that extent* you will want sooner." Thus it appears that the first *the* has a relative force, and the second *the* a demonstrative force.

196. An interrogative adverb introduces a question.

Where, when, whence, whither, how, why, may be used as **interrogative adverbs**. Thus,—

Where are you going?

Why must you go?

COMPARISON OF ADVERBS

197. Adverbs have three degrees of comparison,—the positive, the comparative, and the superlative.

1. Most adverbs are compared by means of *more* and *most*.

> John came *promptly*. [Positive.]
>
> Richard came *more promptly* than John. [Comparative.]
>
> Henry came *most promptly* of all. [Superlative.]

2. A few adverbs are compared by means of the endings *er* and *est*. Thus,—

Positive	Comparative	Superlative
near	nearer	nearest
soon	sooner	soonest

Further examples are:— cheap, dear, early, fast, hard, high, long, loud, quick, slow, deep.[25]

Some adverbs are compared in both ways. Thus,—

> often, oftener *or* more often, oftenest *or* most often.

198. Several adverbs have irregular comparison.

Positive	Comparative	Superlative
far	farther	farthest
forth	further	furthest

ill	worse	worst
badly		
nigh	nigher	nighest
		next
well	better	best
late	later	latest
		last
little	less	least
much	more	most

These adverbs in the main have the same forms as the adjectives studied in § 185 above. Note, however: (1) that *good* and *bad* are never adverbs; (2) that *ill* and *well, better* and *best, worse* and *worst,* may be either adverbs or adjectives. *Rather* is now used in the comparative only.

USE OF THE COMPARATIVE AND SUPERLATIVE

199. The comparative degree, not the superlative, is used in comparing two persons or things.

The superlative is used in comparing one person or thing with two or more.

RIGHT:
Mary is the *more agreeable* of the two.

Mary is the *most agreeable* of all the family.

I like both Mary and Jane, but I am *fondest* of Mary.

WRONG:
I am studying Latin, history, and geometry, but I dislike the *latter.*

The same principle applies to adverbs.

John runs *faster* than Tom. [Here the acts of two persons are compared.]

Which of you three can run *fastest*? [Here the acts of more than two are compared.]

NOTE. In older English the superlative sometimes occurs when only two objects are thought of. This use is still found in a few proverbial phrases: as,—"Put your *best* foot *foremost.*"

200. The superlative is sometimes used merely for emphasis, without implying any definite comparison: as—"My *dearest* Kate!"

The superlative of emphasis is very common with *most.*

Most potent, grave, and *reverend* signiors.—SHAKSPERE.

Justice had been *most cruelly* defrauded.—WORDSWORTH.

Excessive use of this construction (like frequent repetition of *very*) is tiresome and weakens style. Double comparison (as *more worthier, most unkindest*) is common in older English, but is now a gross error.

201. When two adjectives or adverbs are contrasted by means of *than, more* is used with the first.

Such indulgence is *more kind* than wise.

This scheme is *more clever* than honest.

He acts *more boldly* than discreetly.

NOTE. The adverb *rather* is often used with the first adjective or adverb (as,—"*rather* kind than wise" or "kind *rather* than wise"), but in a slightly different sense.

202. Many adjectives and adverbs are, from their meaning, incapable of comparison. Such are:—

1. Adjectives expressing a quality as absolute or complete, and adverbs derived from such adjectives.

EXAMPLES: unique, universal, single, matchless, instantaneous, triangular, everlasting, infinite, mortal; uniquely, singly, eternally, mortally.

2. The adverbs *here, there, then, now, when*, and the like.

NOTE. Words like *perfect, exact, straight*, etc., are commonly said to be incapable of comparison, but this is an error. For each of these words may vary in sense. When *perfect* (for example) denotes *absolute perfection*, it cannot be compared. But *perfect* has also another sense: namely, "partaking in a higher or lower degree of the qualities that make up absolute perfection," so that we may describe one statue as *more perfect* than another, or one of three statues as the *most perfect* of them all. In this use, which is unobjectionable, we simply admit that nothing in the world is absolutely flawless, and assert that the three statues approach ideal perfection in various degrees.

203. An adjective phrase may sometimes be compared by means of *more* and *most*.

I was never *more out of humor* [= more vexed].

I think your last suggestion *most in keeping* [= most appropriate].

NUMERALS—ADJECTIVES, NOUNS, AND ADVERBS

204. Words indicating number are called numerals. They are adjectives, nouns, or adverbs.

There are *seven* days in the week. [Adjective.]
Twelve make a *dozen*. [Noun.]
I have called *twice*. [Adverb.]

205. The chief classes of numerals are **cardinals** and **ordinals**.

1. **Cardinal numeral adjectives (*one, two, three, four*, etc.) are used in counting, and answer the question "How many?"**

I had to pay *three* dollars.

There were *forty-two* vessels in the fleet.

NOTE. In such expressions as "The boy was *sixteen*," the numeral is a predicate adjective limiting *boy* (§ 172, 3). We need not expand *sixteen* to "sixteen years old."

2. Ordinal numeral adjectives (*first, second, third,* etc.) denote the position or order of a person or thing in a series.

Carl plays the *second* violin.

Your friend is sitting in the *fifth* row.

206. All the cardinal and ordinal numerals may become nouns and may take a plural ending in some of their senses.

One is enough.

Four are missing.

The *nine* played an excellent game.

Three *twos* are six.

The men formed by *fours*.

Thousands perished by the way.

Eight is two *thirds* of twelve. [So regularly in **fractional parts**.]

NOTE. *Hundred, thousand, million* were originally nouns, but are now equally common as adjectives. Other numeral nouns are:—twain, couple, pair, brace, trio, quartette, quintette, foursome, dozen, score, century.

207. Certain numeral adjectives (*single, double, triple,* etc.) indicate how many times a thing is taken or of how many like parts it consists.

A *double* row of policemen stood on guard.

A *fourfold* layer of chilled steel forms the door.

Some of these words may be used as adverbs.

The cabman charged *double*.

His fear increased *tenfold*.

208. Certain numeral adverbs and adverbial phrases indicate how many times an action takes place.

Once my assailant slipped.

I rang the bell *twice*.

The river hath *thrice* flow'd, no ebb between.—Shakspere.

The only adverbs of this kind in ordinary use are *once* and *twice*. For larger numbers an adverbial phrase (*three times, four times,* etc.) is employed. *Thrice,* however, is still common in poetry and the solemn style.

9 781805 476641